BRITISH BATTLEFIELDS by Philip Warner
Volume 1 – The South

WHERE BATTLES WERE FOUGHT
WHY THEY WERE FOUGHT
HOW THEY WERE WON AND LOST

Index Of Battles

INTRODUCTION

Very few living men have taken part in a battle, and many must wonder how they would acquit themselves if ever they had to.

A medieval battle was a very complex affair; it was far from being a simple matter of kill or be killed. It could be won or lost at any stage; it could turn on the action of one man, and not necessarily a man of high rank either, and it could settle nothing, or alternatively the fate of a nation.

But for the majority, when thinking of a battle, the overriding question would be: how would I behave? What would happen to me? Would I emerge unscathed and join in the celebrations, or would I be left wounded on the battlefield waiting for someone to save me, or for some ghoul to finish me off? Would I lose all fear in the excitement?

In reading the descriptions in this book it may be possible to guess the answers to some of those questions. On some of these battlefields you may feel luckier than on others. When you visit them it is worth bearing in mind that your own relations fought on these fields. This is almost certain. Everyone has two parents, four grandparents, sixteen great-grandparents ...and so on. If you work this out you may be sure that in any battle described in these books you probably had a number of ancestors fighting on each side. Doubtless they held a wide variety of ranks.

What were your chances? Battles are very strange. A wise commander does not give battle till he is sure he can win; some do not do so until they feel they have won already. Even today your estimate of why a former battle was won may be as good as anyone else's, for it is a strange fact about battles that often men do not know why they were won. The fact that one side had more casualties than the other means little. Most of the slaughter took place when one side had decided all was lost. The number killed when the battle was being fought may be small.

In examining these battlefields, and assessing the general situation, you must put yourself in the position of one of the senior commanders. You must remember how many troops you have and consider their quality. Are they well-trained, and well-armed? If not, are they well led? Do the junior commanders know their job? Will they keep their heads, take their men to the right objectives, control them in apparent victory, rally them in apparent defeat? Are they all going to be in their right places at the right time? What are their weapons like? Are the men skilled in their use? Many hundred years ago, in the declining years of the Roman Empire, a strategist wrote: 'A handful of men inured to war proceed to certain victory, while on the contrary numerous armies of raw and undisciplined troops are but multitudes of men dragged to slaughter.' It is as true today as it was then.

There were fashions in warfare, just as there were fashions in everything else, and sometimes a military fashion could be as impracticable as any other. On occasion armies were defeated because their commanders were relentlessly obstinate about moving with the times. In the first battle of this book we shall see how cavalry and bowmen won a battle against infantrymen but this led to an over-emphasis on the value of cavalry and neglect of infantry.

The axe was despised by the Normans because the Saxons used it, but became a very fashionable weapon for Normans later. The doom of the armoured knight eventually came from the longbow which was in use at the time of Hastings but in remote parts of Wales only. Whatever plans commanders make for battle they are -as often as not - thrown into disarray by unpredictable happenings on both sides. Confusion soon settles down on a battlefield and it is the commander who in that fast-changing, dangerous situation can think constructively and clearly who wins. The atmosphere of muddle which settles on to a battlefield is known as 'the fog of war'. The terms 'strategy' and 'tactics' are used loosely nowadays, and applied to so many non-military matters, that their proper meaning tends to be blurred. Strategy means the overall plan of a campaign for the defeat of an army, nation and people. Strategy requires you to mobilize all your resources, not only of people but also of food and weapons and equipment. It involves organizing the use of land, sea, and air transport, the use of propaganda, the preparation of de- tailed plans for a campaign and the provision of contingency plans against the unexpected. Just as it tries to organize its own resources it will try to disorganize the opposition. Nowadays, propaganda designed to upset enemy morale can be disseminated through radio, press and television. In the past it was done by spreading rumours through infiltrators. Rumours - particularly of bad news - spread very rapidly. The most morale-destroying rumour is that the commander-in-chief has prematurely departed from the field. In at least two of the battles described here commanders killed their horses at the outset with a view to showing that they themselves would stay to the end, whatever the probable result.

Strategy might or might not be influenced by the nature of the ground; tactics undoubtedly would be. Tactics is the science of the layout of troops in the face of the enemy and their use in action. Minor tactics deals with the problems occurring to sub-units, which maybe of patrol strength. However, it must not be thought that minor tactics are of little account. Skill in minor tactics is vital to success in a campaign. Strategy and tactics were not invariably the reason why battles were fought, for some occurred by accident; but strategy, if not tactics, brought the opposing armies to the point at which battle was joined. Both were in turn influenced by the physical features of the countryside. Very often these might be overlooked. It is obvious that armies have to take into account; mountains, hills, rivers, roads, swamps, forest, or very rough ground. What is less obvious is the influence of much smaller physical features. The battle of Poitiers in France 1356 was won by the Black Prince because the English could not be dislodged from a twenty-foot high hill protected by a hedge and a ditch; at the battle of Agincourt in 1415 the French lost because they tried to advance over newly-ploughed fields which were sodden from the recent rains. But battles may be lost for even less obvious reasons. A tree might serve as a rallying point, as an observation post, or as the cause of the split in the advance of an army; a stream might enable an army and its horses to refresh themselves, or might lead to its defeat. When on a battlefield it is advisable to look for every tiny rivulet and patch of marshy ground. As that rivulet was trampled in and clogged with bodies it could soon become a marsh, and then a miniature lake. Woe betide anyone who was pushed back into it, particularly if he was wearing heavy armour. On some battlefields you will find a site marked 'Bloody Meadow'. A glance at the surrounding topography will show how it obtained its chilling name.

A stream might have been damned before the battle began in order to make the enemy advance on a very narrow front. This would nullify an advantage in numbers. During the Zulu wars in the nineteenth century a handful of Dutch held back thousands of Zulus because the latter could not reach them; the place was subsequently known as 'Blood River'. Kenilworth Castle, which does not look particularly formidable today, was once made impregnable by the damning of two small streams; it was then surrounded by 111 acres of water.

Control of an area is made effective by a commander being able to move forces rapidly from one part to another. Thus you will find battlefields near roads or rivers, or *nodal points* as junctions of either are called. For the same reason you will find the entrance to valleys, or passes, or bridges and fords, all bear traces of nearby fortifications. It is all too easy to underrate these fortifications because many people merely see them as inert defences which would be dangerous within arrow range only. On the contrary they were bases, and although built to give a good account of themselves if besieged, would mainly be used to house fighters who would tackle the opposition just as they emerged out of the river or perhaps before they were in sight of the fortification. The problem of a fortification, however small, to an advancing army, was that it would be too great a threat yet might take time to reduce. And time might be a vital commodity. Delay might prevent an army reaching a vital river crossing before it was strongly defended, might prevent it from capturing a town which held vital stores, or might prevent a link-up with other forces, converging from different directions.

The sites of battles are then anything but haphazard. But before being able to predict why and where battles must have been fought you need to investigate what changes have taken place in the countryside between the date of the battle and today. It may surprise you. What is now dry ploughland may once have been wet tussocky scrubland, the battlefield may perhaps have a town built on it but even then there are probably tell-tale signs. But even if the surface of the battlefield has been largely obliterated the surrounding area will do much to explain it. You will soon learn to recognise the importance of certain features- or 'develop an eye for ground'. With a little practice you will be able to estimate where the attack came from before even looking at the detailed map. You will make mistakes. You will perhaps forget the time it takes to move men over encumbered ground; it is no good saying 'he should have attacked on the flank' if the approach would have been thick with bodies and abandoned equipment. You will probably try to squeeze too many men into too small an area- as many a commander has done before you. You will perhaps neglect your cavalry, or your artillery. In assessing what you yourself might have done you must accept completely what the enemy did do. Your version of the battle may prove more successful than your predecessor's - or less.

Battles, in the times we speak of, lasted but a day. Pursuit and slaughter may have taken longer but the decision would be reached in a matter of hours. Siege battles were, of course, a different story. The explanation of the shortness of early battles lies in the weapons they used. Draw a bow a hundred times and see how much longer you want to go on for. Take a sword, or a billhook, and try hacking a way through a copse for an hour.

Better still, pad yourself up with protective clothing before you begin and move rapidly from place to place. Even then you will lack the noise, the effect of cavalry changes sending a shock through the ranks, and the bruises that often came from the weapons of friends as well as foes.

But you will be getting the feel of a medieval battle.

The Battle of Hastings
10th October 1066

Most people have heard of the Battle of Hastings, and know that it was fought in 1066. What is known beyond that usually tends to be wrong or, at least, misinterpreted. The general impression is that the true Englishman King Harold was defeated - somewhat unfairly - by a foreigner who had no right to be in England at all.

The facts are as follows. The Battle of Hastings was not fought at Hastings but at Battle, which lies six and three-quarter miles to the north-west. The site is also known to some as Senlac, which means 'a sandy brook'; the term Senlac Hill which is sometimes used is therefore confused.

The Normans who conquered the Anglo-Saxons (1) at Hastings were not, as is generally supposed, the first Normans to set foot in this country. Edward the Confessor, who reigned from 1042 to 1066 was almost more of a Norman than an Englishman. He himself came of the Anglo-Saxon family descended from Alfred the Great but as the Danes had overrun the country Saxon heirs to the throne had to live in exile or lose their heads. When the last Danish king died in 1042 Edward was brought back from Normandy, where he had virtually forgotten the Anglo-Saxon language, and made king.

1 The Anglo-Saxons will henceforward be referred to as 'Saxons' in this account of the battle.

Edward then became an ineffective king at a time when the country was desperately in need of firm government. For most of his reign he was either overawed by the powerful Saxon Earl Godwin or duped by his own Norman favourites. When Godwin died his son Harold took over his posts and his influence. Harold was a brave and able governor of England and also made himself well- respected in Scotland and Wales. The story of Macbeth is well- enough known; it was Harold who organized his defeat and the restoration of the true heirs to the Scottish throne. In Wales Harold personally led an expedition which chased the Welsh king to the heights of Snowdon; there he was decapitated by his followers and his head brought to Harold's feet. This was the type of man Harold was: awe-inspiring, brave, experienced, and respected.

William was no less of a warrior. His upbringing had been harsh and dangerous. He was the bastard son of the Duke of Normandy by a tanner's daughter; it is said that his father first saw his mother when she was washing in a stream. Later she was married off to a suitable husband and had other distinguished sons. Bastardy was no hindrance to succession in Norman law, and William succeeded to the dukedom of Normandy at the age often; that he survived and grew to manhood and great power was due to a large measure of luck. Much of his childhood was spent in avoiding being assassinated; much of his early maturity was spent in desperate fighting to obtain a grip on his dukedom, and protect it from his ambitious neighbours. His claim to the throne of England was marginally stronger than that of Harold, who had no blood connection. However, when Edward the Confessor died the Saxon Council (the Witan) had no hesitation in electing Harold as their king. He was on the spot, he had virtually ruled the country for the last fourteen years, and he was apparently recommended by the dying Edward. There was, in fact, another candidate in Edward's great nephew Edgar Aetheling but as he was only ten nobody paid any attention to his claim.

The situation was further complicated by the fact that under duress Harold had been tricked into swearing he would support William's claims. (1) Yet another problem for Harold was the fact that he had much jealousy to contend with in the north of his kingdom.

(1) He had once agreed to support William, when, after a shipwreck, he had fallen into William's power in Normandy

Harold was not a 'lucky' commander. He won battles by courage and technical brilliance; the succession of events which brought his death at Senlac would not have happened to a lucky man.

The first piece of bad luck was the broken oath to support William. Although an oath under duress it was an oath none the less. This meant that the force which William brought to England had a papal blessing and his men believed they would win because they were fighting a usurper and an oath-breaker. Morale has always been a vital factor in battles but never more so than in medieval warfare; on this occasion morale was boosted by the religious nature of the invasion, but also by the thought of the magnificent plunder which success would bring.

The battle took place on 14 October 1066. Six months earlier William had begun assembling an invasion army and the fleet to carry it. Harold was well aware of these preparations and had maintained a coast watch throughout the summer. Military service was then supplied by the 'fyrd' system, by which men were called up for two months at a time. In September the weather was cold and blustery; it looked as if winter would soon make invasion impossible. The most critical time for a country fearing invasion is when the harvest has been gathered and before winter has set in. Readers may recall that 'Operation Sealion', the German plan to invade Britain in the autumn of 1940 was cancelled by Hitler on 12 October; this was because the German Air Force had failed to establish air superiority before rough weather made the crossing of the Channel with invasion barges impracticable.

Unfortunately for Harold, on 15 September 1066, the King of Norway made a surprise landing in Yorkshire. (On 15 September 1940 the Battle of Britain was won in the air.)

Hardrada, King of Norway, also had a claim to the English throne although neither he nor anyone else took it very seriously. However, in the previous year, Harold had made an unfortunate diplomatic mistake. His younger brother, Tostig, had been made Earl of Northumbria by Edward the Confessor. It was a bad appointment, based entirely on a personal whim, and this was shown when the district rebelled against the new earl. Harold, having looked into the matter, advised Edward to banish Tostig, and in his place approved the appointment of Morcar. Northumbria was then much more than Northumberland is today and comprised roughly what the name suggests - the district north of the Humber. This substantial favour in no way diminished Morcar's envy and jealousy of Harold, and eventually contributed to the loss of the Battle of Hastings. Morcar's feelings were shared by his brother Eadwine, who controlled Mercia, as the central provinces of England were then called. This feeling of jealousy and antagonism was eventually expressed by the brothers' failure to hurry support to Harold against William's invasion. Five years after the conquest they received their just reward; one was killed in a skirmish and the other was imprisoned for life.

But in 1066 the nemesis of Eadwine and Morcar was far distant. As Harold was waiting for the inevitable invasion from Normandy he suddenly heard that a more immediate danger was present in the north. Tostig, raging at the loss of his earldom, had gone to Norway and enlisted the aid of Hardrada the King of Norway. The Vikings were a formidable people; they fought for the pure love of fighting, fear did not exist for them, and they took no heed at all of the occasional disasters which overtook them on land and sea. But of all the Viking raiders - and there had been many - none was so famed and feared as Hardrada. He was reputed to be seven feet tall - and this could have been true, for some of the Vikings were veritable giants- but whatever his stature there was no question of his ability. Tostig had no difficulty in enlisting his aid; it was a fight with the plunder of the kingdom to follow. They embarked in 300 ships.

Morcar and Eadwine were the first to meet the onslaught but their forces were brushed aside with wholesale slaughter, at Fulford, near the gates of York. Morcar and Eadwine did not stay to see the eventual results of the fight, which would doubtless include the capture and sacking of the city; they had previously moved out of the danger area. However, in this case, the early departure of the chiefs from the battlefield probably did not demonstrate lack of personal courage but merely a frantic desire to rally other resistance. Among the qualifications for military command, at any level, complete absence of fear was always assumed. Even if the fear was not absent - and it seldom is - the commander would never show it. This assumption is as marked and important today as ever it was. In previous centuries this absolute freedom from fear has always been considered a natural prerogative of the aristocracy, a man-at-arms, or a peasant might be as brave as his lord, but none could be braver. Then, as now, good units had both individual and collective courage. As Napoleon said of his veterans at Waterloo 'They will not run away and it will take a long time to kill them all.' The Vikings, and their descendants the Normans (originally 'the North- men') probably felt no fear, only excitement. They were possessed with 'berserkgangr' - joy in battle, which made them at their happiest when fighting; they probably approached a bloody conflict with the same feelings which modern man does a game of football.

The battle for York had taken place on 20 September and the disastrous news was brought promptly to Harold; even more promptly he acted. Having heard of the landing a day or two previously he was already on his way to the north but time prevented him from collecting more than 3,000 men against the invaders' 6,000. He reached York on 25 September and pushed on to meet the invaders in the dawn of the next day at Stamford Bridge, seven miles from York. Hardrada and Tostig were caught unprepared for the sudden onslaught and hardly had time to take up their proper fighting formation. There was a dramatic 'Horatio holds the bridge' scene when they had retreated across the Derwent, for the single bridge was held by a formidable Viking. Unlike Horatio, this intrepid warrior who was holding up the entire Saxon army, did not save the bridge; he was stabbed from below by an equally hardy Saxon who had floated himself under that part of the bridge on which the Viking was standing.

The battle of Stamford Bridge lasted for a few hours only and it must have been one of the bloodiest of all battles. Apart from the shield wall favoured by Saxon and Viking alike there seems to have been little in the way of tactics. Hardrada and Tostig were both killed and the remnants of the force which had required 300 ships to bring it in was glad to slip away in twenty-four, possibly some 500 men in all. It seems unlikely that the rest can all have been killed in a few hours' battle but fugitives would have had short shrift in those times. However, the day after Stamford Bridge saw the Norman invasion force cross the Channel. It had been held up for a month by contrary winds, a circumstance which caused William much trouble and anxiety. But with the change of wind William's star was undoubtedly in the ascendant: the fyrd had been disbanded, Harold's own fleet had just put in to London for a refit leaving the crossing unopposed, and Harold and his army were in the middle of Yorkshire.

Harold did not, in fact, learn that the Normans had landed until 2 October. But again he lost no time. The southern fyrd was called up and began to move towards Pevensey, which was where the Normans had landed. Harold set off south on a forced march with his army. They were an elite force. The housecarles were a personal bodyguard, and the officers were thegns - that is, landowners who were men of substance, rank, and responsibility. Unfortunately, as a fighting machine it was slightly out of date.

The Norman force which had established itself in Sussex was a better balanced and more modern army. In quality it was probably inferior to Harold's Saxons but it had two useful assets which the Saxons lacked; it had cavalry and it had archers. In all the army probably numbered 9,000, of which one-third were armoured knights or mounted troopers. Transporting the horses had been a considerable problem; some had not stood the journey well, and if William had not been extremely fortunate in the weather there is a strong chance that his cavalry would have lost him the battle before it even began. It was not a very sophisticated army for they had little idea of manoeuvre. Their general technique was to charge their opponents, lay about them with sword and mace and hope to make a breach in the line which could be exploited by foot soldiers. The latter carried a variety of lesser arms which included spears, slings, swords and bows. The bowmen were not very highly rated; they had short bows which they drew to the chest; these were in no way comparable to the formidable crossbows and longbows of later years. Still, anyone who has ever used a bow - and most people have - know that it does not require much of a weapon to send a sharp arrow a distance of some seventy yards. Later bows managed five or six times that distance.

It is believed that here were a few archers among the Saxons too, but not enough to have much effect. Most of Harold's army were armed with axes, which they used with fearful strength and precision. They could split an adversary to his chest or lop off a limb with easy skill. Some had short-handled axes which they might throw - in the Frankish tradition, and there was a wide variety of crude but deadly implements, a scythe, a billhook or a spear are formidable weapons in the hands of an experienced and skilled user. However, if you are handling a weapon which you swing, and which depends very much on the velocity of that swing, it means that your body armour must be light, flexible, and therefore not a great protection. By contrast, the Normans could wear chain mail and carry long shields. The chain mail was simple, consisting of rings sewn on to leather but it kept its wearer out of much trouble. There was always a delicate balance in these matters. Either you fought with light weapons and minimal armour, relying on speed and agility for effectiveness, or you transformed yourself into a sort of land battleship, heavy, slow, difficult to conquer, but by no means invulnerable.

Having heard the bad news of the Norman landing on 2 October Harold set off south with a substantial contingent immediately. He arrived in London by nightfall of the sixth, a journey of just under 200 miles in six days. This was an excellent but by no means exceptional achievement. In medieval warfare men were often required to make forced marches, and were well-accustomed to long and awkward journeys. The powers of endurance of the medieval soldier have been scarcely recognized but they were obviously almost superhuman by many modern standards. However, in World War II, the Special Air Service, which sent raiders deep behind the German lines in the desert, achieved similar standards. As an example one man walked 180 miles alone, without food and with very little water, and part of the way without boots (Private Sillito in 1942). There were other performances hardly less remarkable. Doubtless many medieval soldiers would not have found them remarkable at all.

The general impression that Harold marched north to defeat Hardrada, and then promptly marched straight back to Hastings where he was defeated because of exhaustion is incorrect. He spent four days in London collecting his forces and arranging his army. He should have waited longer, for Morcar and Eadwine had not yet joined him because of jealousy and stupidity, and the western contingents had not had sufficient time to march in. But Harold would not wait. It was said that this was because he did not like the reports he heard of Kent and Sussex being pillaged by the Normans but it is more likely that he was over-confident and longing to get to grips with William. On the eleventh he left London.

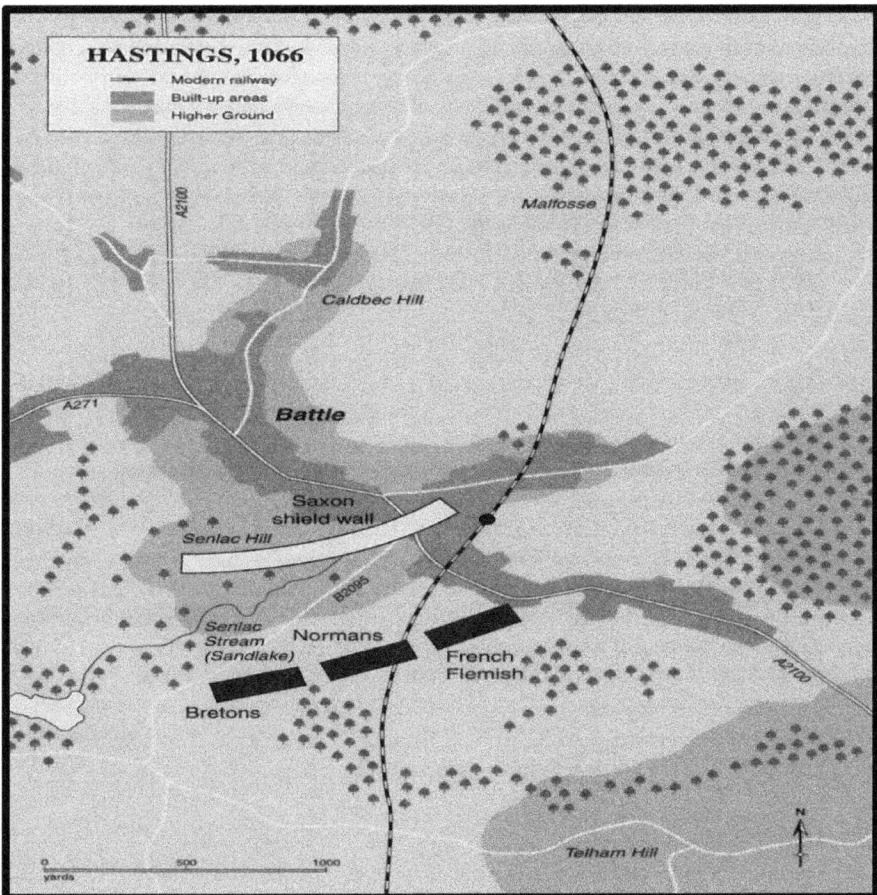

HASTINGS, 1066

— Modern railway
Built-up areas
Higher Ground

Malfosse

Caldbec Hill

Battle

Saxon shield-wall

Senlac Hill

Senlac Stream (Sandlake)

Normans

French Flemish

Bretons

Telham Hill

0   500   1000
yards

The battle site is partly built on by Battle Abbey (which provides excellent guides). The Norman viewpoint is best seen from the B2095 road. The main features of the battlefield are clearly discernible (East Sussex).

The site he chose for the battle cannot be faulted. In order to reach London William would have had to march along a ridge which extends nearly seven miles north-west of Hastings. Just before the ridge reaches Senlac it drops; the traveller therefore has to cross a valley and climb a steep slope on the farther side. On that slope Harold deployed his army. It was broad enough to make a flank attack difficult, and had the added advantage of a wooded region in the rear in case the Saxons were driven back from the slopes. The bottom of the valley was marshy, from the Senlac stream. Senlac or 'Senlache' meaning 'sandy stream'. The point was apparently marked by a 'hoar apple tree' but subsequently William established an abbey on the spot, placing the High Altar on the place where Harold was killed. The hill itself is 1,100 yards long by 150 yards wide. It was clearly a point of great strategic importance and had doubtless been known as such for centuries. It is fifty-seven miles from London and Harold had covered the distance in three days. As a march it bore no comparison with the trek up north and back again but fifty-seven miles in three days in full battle kit scarcely leaves a man at his freshest. As the battle took place on the fourteenth it was obvious that Harold had to occupy the site or subsequently fight in a much less favourable situation.

One point will never be resolved. Harold may have been pressing forward to destroy the Normans around Pevensey and Hastings but might have halted for the night in a good defensive position. Alternatively he may have been warned that the Normans had abandoned their destructive activities in Sussex and were now marching towards London; if so he had to meet them in a defensive position which was ideal for the purpose.

Today the upper part and crest of the hill is occupied by Battle Abbey but it is possible to walk over most of it. There are a number of guides who will give a full account of 1066 and subsequent history. It is possible, without too much walking to view the battlefield from both Saxon and Norman positions. The local museum, in the middle of the town and almost opposite the Abbey gateway, has an excellent relief plan of the battlefield with the disposition of the opposing troops.

It was said - by the Norman chroniclers - that the Saxons spent the night before the battle in feasting, and the Normans spent it in praying; neither seems particularly likely. One account says that the Saxons dug themselves in with a trench protected by stakes, but this may have been a misunderstanding of what was meant by the 'shield wall'. Whatever their nocturnal activities it seems that it took a considerable time for them to get into battle array on the fourteenth, for the battle does not seem to have begun till 9 a.m. - or perhaps even later. The numbers were probably approximately even, about 9,000 each. On the Norman side about 3,000 were mounted, armoured in chain mail. There was some chain mail among the foot soldiers also.

The Saxon army comprised an elite force of housecarles, probably numbering 2,000. These held the centre, and fought with axes. On the flanks were the less well-armed levies of the *fyrd.* The latter had a wide assortment of weapons, including spears and bows. The Saxons possessed horses, and often rode them to battle but would fight dismounted. They were in a good position on top of the ridge; they were blocking the road to London at a point where either side was marshy, where the slope was steep enough to take the edge off any cavalry charges, and where any retreat would draw the invader into a particularly dangerous piece of forest. However, Harold never contemplated retreat or luring the Normans into an ambush. He planned to fight it out where they stood, and in fact came very close to victory by that method.

The Norman army was drawn up in the pattern which became standard practice later, that is, in 'battles', which were oblong divisions. Each battle was made up of a front of archers, a centre of foot soldiers and a rear of armoured knights. Anyone who changed his mind about wanting to be in the hottest part of the battle would have little scope, for if he turned to flee he would be chopped down by his own side. Once a man was committed to a medieval battlefield it was undoubtedly 'death or victory', unless he was of such high rank that his ransom would be so valuable that the enemy would do their best to take him alive. William arranged his army with Bretons on the left, with Normans under his personal command in the centre, and with French and Flemings on the right. William had surveyed the position from Telham Hill, behind his centre, and perhaps retired to that observation point at intervals in the battle. Harold's command post is marked today at Battle, and is a few yards from the spot where he finally fell.

As the Norman army moved forward a jester named Taillefer rode out in front, anxious to strike the first blow. He succeeded, but in a few moments was killed. The armies paused for a second to watch, then set-to themselves. The Norman archers launched off a few flights of arrows but these inflicted very little damage. As they came close together there was a shower of spears from either side but these too had slight effect; the Saxon shield wall remained unbroken and the Normans still pressed forward. When they came to close quarters the real bloodshed began; the Normans hacked away with sword and lance while the housecarles swept their formidable axes like flails and cut through armour and man.

The tremendous power of the Saxon axe blows sliced cleanly through the Norman mail and took off an arm or leg in a blow. The charges of the Norman cavalry were perhaps more of a novelty than a threat, for their horses were light, and there was little tactical plan, so after a while they fell back and let their infantry get on with the work; their own time would come later. William had three horses killed under him during the battle, though at what stage is not known, and there were doubtless other Norman knights who were equally surprised at their reception. The Normans hoped to batter holes in the shield wall; the Saxons on the other hand were prepared to chop all comers to pieces. The slaughter at close quarters was a little too much for the Bretons on the Norman left and they fell back. In doing so they exposed the left flank of the Norman battle in the centre, and this column too began to retire. In the confusion William was lost to sight and the rumour- quick to spread in such circumstances- was that he was dead. He was equally quick to dispel it and pulled off his helmet as he stood up in his stirrups and shouted angrily at those around him. They steadied, and as soon as they did so William and his half-brother, the notorious and warlike Bishop Odo, put in a cavalry charge on to the Saxons who had come down the slope in pursuit of the Bretons .For a while all was confusion and then it was seen that the Saxons were giving way under this unexpected onslaught. As we see in other battles in this book there were few incidents more destructive to morale than a heavy cavalry charge on their flanks just when men thought they were proceeding to victory. Well-organized infantry with pikes, and training in handling them, would be a match for cavalry but on disorganized troops the effect of cavalry can be devastating. Some of the Saxons fought to the death on the mound to the left; the remainder straggled back up the hill to their comrades. It had been an ugly moment for both sides and it came after continuous fighting when neither side was in a fit state to take proper advantage of the situation. There was a lull while both sides recovered breath and prepared for the next grim onslaught.

When it came the Normans were committing their whole force and tried time and again to break into the Saxon line. But the line held and as the bodies mounted it was the Normans who at times fell back. Clearly they could not have fought continuously, and as the Normans occasionally withdrew the Saxons pushed forward in spite of their earlier experience. Subsequently the chroniclers described these minor retreats as tactical devices to break up the Saxon formation but this is unlikely.

But the Saxon line was shrinking. Perhaps they should have gone on to the attack and driven at the heart of the Norman position. As it was they stood on the defensive, which is never very helpful to morale. It is said that some of the fyrd were losing heart and slipped away. Whatever the reason, the line of housecarles became shorter and became a semi-circle around Harold.

At that moment the Normans, who had sent back to Pevensey for more arrows, had a stroke of luck. Knowing that the arrows could not penetrate the shield wall they sent them high in the air from close range. Whether one hit Harold in the eye or not is not known. A piece of the Bayeux tapestry, on which much of our knowledge of the battle is based, gives the impression that an arrow is either passing Harold 's head or penetrating it. His brothers were already dead; his faithful thegns were close around him but they must have been few in numbers. The chances are that most of the fyrd had fallen back to lose itself in the shelter of the trees in the gathering dusk, and the housecarles, who had borne the brunt of the battle, were fighting almost alone. But they fought on, even when Harold was wound ed. Finally a party of Norman knights broke through the last cordon and stabbed the dying king. One, in fact, stabbed him after he was dead, and was disgraced for what was considered a coward's blow. Harold was heavily cut about and his corpse was so disfigured that it could only be identified by his mistress - Edith Swan-neck. Those thegns who were not killed fled overseas. Their possessions were forfeit if they had been at Hastings and many of them joined the Varangian Guard, the elite corps at Byzantium.

Even when the battle was over the Normans nearly met disaster pursuing the remaining Saxon, some of the cavalry had ridden on recklessly in the dusk. The ground behind the Saxon position is rough today, and then would undoubtedly have been more so, as well as being covered with trees. At some point behind the Saxon position, mentioned in the chronicles as 'Malfosse' (the evil ditch) the Normans ran into disaster. Probably some of them broke their necks on the steep slopes of Caldbec Hill, or were ambushed in the forest. In any event some of them panicked and were fleeing back to Senlac until they were once more rallied.

One day's battle had won a kingdom, for there was no other major battle; and London surrendered after William had made an encircling movement. Afterwards he held down the land with motte and bailey castles, with sheriffs, and laws, and feudal obligation. By parcelling out the land into manors, and making the owners rent it by military service he gave himself an army with a vested interest in his survival. When the conquered gave trouble - as they did in Devon and Yorkshire - he destroyed them, their horses, and their crops. Appropriately he met his own death twenty-one years later when his horse trod on a burning beam in a French town he was sacking, and fatally injured him by throwing against the high pommel of his saddle.

The Normans who won the Battle of Hastings had short hair and shaven faces; the Saxons had long hair and moustaches. Before many years, however, the Normans were also growing their hair long and appearing with moustaches, although much criticized by their priests and leaders for doing so. The controversy about hair is as old as the British nation. (1)

(1) It is often thought that the Anglo-Saxons were a brutal and uncivilized people and that the Normans were culturally far more advanced. Archaeologists have evidence which refutes this.

After William had won the battle he took a vow to build an abbey with the High Altar on the spot where Harold fell. He honoured his oath, and the foundations may be seen to this day, although the abbey which now stands on Senlac Hill is of much later date. The tree known as Harold's oak (actually a beech) is, of course, later still. Unfortunately, few other traces of the battle remain for the surface has risen. Perhaps one day deep excavation will bring relics to light.

The battle inspired many Normans to lyrical prose but some of their description may owe more to enthusiasm than to fact:

There was a French soldier of noble mien, who sat his horse gallantly. He spied two Englishmen who were also carrying themselves boldly. They were both men of great worth and had become companions in arms, and fought together, the one protecting the other.

They bore two long and broad bills, and did great mischief to the Normans, killing both horses and men. The French soldier looked at them and their bills, and was sore alarmed for he was afraid of losing his good horse, the best that he had; and would willingly have turned to some other quarter, if it would not have looked like cowardice. He soon, however, recovered his courage, and spurring his horse gave him the bridle and galloped swiftly forward. Fearing the two bills, he raised his shield, and struck one of the Englishmen with his lance on the breast, so that the iron passed out of his back. At the moment that he fell, the lance broke, and the Frenchman seized the mace that hung at his right side, and struck the other Englishman a blow that completely broke his skull.

On the other side was an Englishman who much annoyed the French, continually assaulting them with a keen-edged hatchet. He had a helmet made of wood, which he had fastened down to his coat, and laced round his neck, so that no blows could reach his head. The ravage he was making was seen by a gallant Norman knight, who rode a large horse that neither fire nor water could stop in its career, when its master urged it on. The knight spurred, and his horse carried him on well till he charged the Englishman, striking him over the helmet, so that it fell down over his eyes; and as he stretched out his hand to raise it, and uncover his face, the Norman cut off his right hand, so that his hatchet fell to the ground. Another Norman sprang forward and eagerly seized the prize with both his hands, but he kept it little space, and paid dearly for it, for as he stopped to pick up the hatchet, an Englishman, with his long-handled axe struck him over the back, breaking all his bones so that his entrails and lungs gushed forth. The knight of the good horse meantime returned without injury; but on his way he met another Englishman, and bore him down under his horse, wounding him grievously, and trampling him altogether under foot. (Wace: Roman de Rou) In one day the pattern of England was established. But as Guizot, the French historian, put it 'England owes her present liberties to being conquered by the Normans.'

THE BATTLE OF LEWES
14 May 1264

After the Battle of Hastings the Normans established an iron grip upon the country which they had conquered in one battle. William I died in 1087 and was succeeded by his dissolute son William II (Rufus the Red). William was a fighter, as a king in those days had to be, but his court, full of homosexuals and harlots, was as corrupt as this country has ever seen. William II was succeeded in 1100 by his brother Henry I, who was noted for lechery, parsimony, and cheerlessness. When Henry died in 1135, leaving a daughter as his heir, anarchy broke out and for nineteen years the country was torn by a civil war in which robber barons did exactly as they pleased to the distress of everyone else. It was known as 'The nineteen long winters when God and his saints slept'. Stephen was eventually succeeded by Henry II, who once more established an iron grip on the country. He is, however, mainly remembered for the careless remark which led to the murder of Thomas a Becket in Canterbury cathedral. Henry II was succeeded by his warlike but absentee son Richard Coeur de Lion, but Richard was killed by a gangrenous arrow wound in 1199 after a ten-year reign, and was succeeded by his brother John. John is one of the most vilified kings in English history but although not an estimable character was probably not as black as he was painted. His reign came to an end in 1216 when he was succeeded by Henry III, who reigned for fifty-six years. Both the beginning and the end of Henry's reign saw trouble, the earlier ones being none of his own fault (he was only nine when he succeeded), but the latter ones entirely due to his own stupidity.

The reign began in civil war because the barons who had rebelled against John had brought over Louis of France to be their potential king. Now that John was dead, and the new king was merely a young boy, there was little point in this rebellion against a tyrant king. But the war was still on and did not come to an end until two considerable battles had been fought; its effects lasted much longer. The country was full of mercenaries and foreigners who had been brought over by John. There were many problems to be resolved, and they were dealt with by Hubert de Burgh until 1227. But after that year Henry was an adult and ruled unadvised except by those who flattered him. He found most of his support in the foreign relations and friends of his wife, Eleanor of Provence. Naturally generous beyond his means Henry went to absurd extremes with these foreign favourites. He even made his wife's uncle, Boniface of Savoy, the Archbishop of Canterbury. Boniface was a young man of no recognizable merit and the appointment was one of extreme irresponsibility. Unfortunately it was typical of many of Henry's actions. He engaged in two futile foreign military enterprises, squandered money recklessly at home and abroad, and appointed foreigners to English posts. (There were 300 Italian priests in lucrative English benefices.) Eventually, when he summoned the Great Council in 1257 and told the barons he needed an enormous grant he found a degree of opposition he had not bargained for. Curiously enough the strength of the opposition was largely due to the personality of a man whom Henry had originally brought from France. This was Simon de Montfort, whose grandmother had been heiress to the earldom of Leicester. The de Montforts were out of favour and had never been allowed the Leicester estates until Henry patronized Simon, married him to his sister, and made him his counsellor. But Henry was too fickle to maintain a long friendship; he soon tired of de Montfort, and sent him abroad to be governor of Guienne. There de Montfort had to use most of his own money in crushing a rebellion and was not reimbursed by Henry. By 1258 de Montfort was an implacable opponent of the English king. As de Montfort was sober, sincere, and competent, he attracted wide-spread support. The result was that Henry was bound by the *Provisions of Oxford* (where the Great Council had met and earned itself the name of 'The Mad Parliament') to govern by the advice of three committees, and to adhere to the principles of Magna Carta. In the ensuing four years Henry tried to strike off baronial control, and eventually was absolved from his oath by the Pope. He then persuaded the barons to accept the King of France as an arbitrator. The latter, in the *Mise of Amiens,* declared he should no longer be bound by the *Provisions of Oxford* although he must act in accord with Magna Carta.

This decision precipitated a civil war for the barons refused to accept the abolition of the restraints imposed by the Provisions. However, their refusal caused some conflict of loyalties and this shifting allegiance would have some influence on the two bloody battles which ensued.

The first of these took place at Lewes on 14May 1264; the second, which reversed it, was fought at Evesham on 4 August 1265.

In the early months of 1264 when it was obvious that a civil war was impending, both sides were organizing their support. Henry had the great earls of Norfolk and Hereford, as well as his own son Prince Edward (who would be the architect of victory at Evesham), about fifty barons, and most of the minor aristocracy. De Montfort had the support of most of the major barons, and probably mustered a greater and better equipped force than his king, though it was not available at Lewes. However, among them were the citizens of London whose indignation at unjust taxation was greater than their military prowess; they were slaughtered wholesale at Lewes. The Londoners had had a fairly good run for their money in the previous five years. They felt that supporting the cause of de Montfort gave them authority to pillage foreign property and massacre Jews. In 1264 they had plundered and destroyed a number of royal possessions. Prince Edward's reckless conduct in pressing on and destroying them at Lewes may well have stemmed from the fact that they had terrified his mother and threatened to drown her as a witch.

Henry began his preparations at Windsor and then raised his banner at Woodstock. He ordered Oxford to be cleared of students; some say it was for their own protection but others think it was because he distrusted their anti-authoritarian attitude. De Montfort planned to muster at Northampton but before he had left Peterborough Prince Edward took the town by a combination of daring on his side and treachery on the other (5 April 1264). Forty royalist knights slipped into the Cluniac priory through a convenient breach in the wall, and the castle was occupied by a subterfuge. The hero of these activities was one Philip Basset, who also distinguished himself at Lewes later by being the last to leave the field although wounded in twenty places. Some of the strongest opposition at Northampton (1) came from the ejected Oxford students who displayed a skill with crossbow and sling worthy of the great classical generals they would otherwise have been studying; they did so much damage that they were lucky not to be put to death in the general massacre which followed the capture of the town.

(1) Northampton Castle, once one of the most impressive in England, was mainly destroyed by the greed of railway speculators in the mid-nineteenth century

De Montfort's son was taken prisoner as were many other valuable supporters. The earl relieved his feelings by returning to London and letting loose a massacre of foreigners and Jews. Meanwhile Leicester and Nottingham surrendered with minimal resistance.
After having left London with no doubt as to who was in control he set off to capture Rochester, which was a royal castle. Rochester had been the scene of a notable siege in the previous reign, and this one looked like being as murderous, for de Montfort employed unusual siege engines and a fireship, but the news that Henry's army was now approaching London caused de Montfort to abandon the attack, leaving a small force to prevent ingress or egress at the castle. But the threat to London had been over-estimated for it was only a probe by Prince Edward, who was very skilled at these alarming opportunist moves. Having set London buzzing, and upset de Montfort's plans, Prince Edward pushed ahead to Rochester and disposed of the small force still investing the castle; he chopped off their hands and feet. Henry could probably have occupied London at this point but instead proceeded to capture the powerful baronial castle at Tonbridge. Having now got a firm grip on the midlands and the south-east Henry decided to move to the west and demolish baronial support on the way. Finally, no doubt, London would be pleased to surrender.

In the event, it did not work out like that. Henry's army had a very trying time from Welsh archers whom de Montfort had thoughtfully sent to harry them. The Welsh, who were the inventors of the longbow, which would win great glory later, were swift, active, and born guerrilla fighters. Using the plentiful cover on the way they did considerable damage to the royal army. Henry was glad to halt at Lewes where the town and castle belonged to John de Warenne, Earl of Surrey. De Montfort, following up, camped some nine miles away and sent a message saying he did not want war but he did require the king to accept the *Provisions of Oxford*. The king did not see this so much as an olive branch as an insult. His rejection said as much. De Montfort, reluctantly, decided to put the issue to battle. He gave orders for the march to Lewes to begin. At Offham village, two miles to the north-west of Lewes he turned off the road and took up position on the hill. Having made an early start he arrived in the early morning and set out his army in three battles with one in reserve. It was a small army in numbers but not in experience; most of his commanders had had experience in French wars, and some in the Crusades. Owing to the disaster of Northampton it was short of cavalry. The Londoners, being of known lesser quality, were mainly in reserve. Three who seemed in need of restraint were locked in a carriage pending disciplinary action. In all probability the opposed forces were roughly equivalent in numbers to those at the Battle of Hastings- 9,000 a side, although de Montfort's army may have been a thousand or two less. Its arrival seems to have taken the royal army by surprise but the latter soon turned out and fell into battle array. Henry commanded the centre, his brother, Richard, Earl of Cornwall, took the left wing, and his son, Prince Edward was on the right, which also included the experienced John de Warenne; the latter however lacked the fighting quality of the other members of his illustrious family.

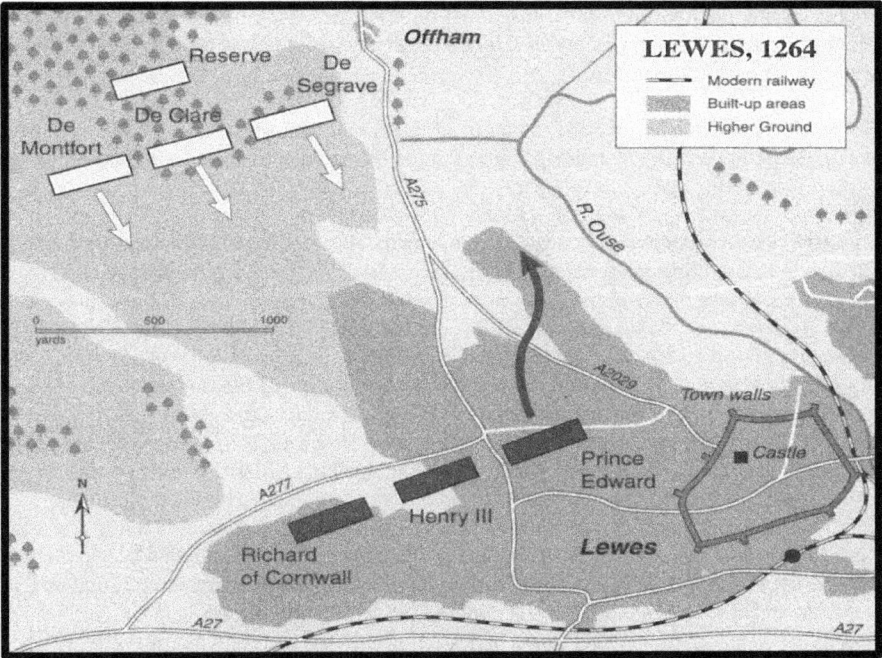

The Royalist view of the battle may be seen from the ramparts of Lewes Castle; the rebel position by climbing the footpath from Offham village (East Sussex).

Tactics showed no improvement on those of Hastings, nearly 200 years before, although military science had improved greatly in the meantime. One account says that de Montfort advanced at a walk until within a hundred yards of the royal force, then ordered a charge. Not wishing to be caught standing when the rebel army had gained momentum the royal army responded with a similar order; the two forces therefore met with a splintering crash. Prince Edward's force on the right soon pushed ahead. The troops opposing were mainly London citizens with no military experience; finding the situation too arduous for them they turned and tried to get out of trouble. Some tried to cross the river (Ouse); others sought shelter in the trees where they felt the royal cavalry would not, or could not, follow. But they were mistaken. Edward and his subordinate commanders, who included a number of Frenchmen, who knew themselves to be heartily detested, never let up. The unfortunate prisoners in de Montfort's carriage were killed before they could explain themselves. Those Londoners who tried to escape across the river were either killed or drowned. As always happened there was a 'bloody meadow' on the river bank where men had hoped to find a ford. Other would-be escapers were slaughtered in Cooksbridge and Halland, and even today it is easy to see why these places proved to be such death traps. It is said that some of the fugitives reached Croydon, some forty miles away, where they had the misfortune to run into another royalist force, and be slaughtered. But the casualties were by no means all on one side. While Edward rushed on in reckless pursuit, much as Prince Rupert did at Edgehill some four hundred years later, a very different story was unfolding elsewhere. De Montfort's centre column was pressing forward steadily towards King Henry's banner, and getting the best of the encounter.

Henry, although fifty-six and not a soldier by inclination, fought well. He is said to have had two horses killed under him and had been battered by sword and mace. Eventually he withdrew from the battle and took shelter in St Pancras priory, which had been founded by the wife of the first Earl of Warenne, soon after the Conquest. His brother, Richard of Cornwall, performed less well. On leaving the field he hid in a windmill where he was surrounded by scoffing de Montfort supporters; however, unlike many, he was allowed to surrender and save his life. Even if you were rich and worth a good ransom in a medieval battle you might not always get away with your life. Tempers ran high; you might be decapitated by an equal in rank or stabbed by some churl who thought he was doing his duty. Fighting went on in various parts of the town but eventually the remnants of the royal army were pursued into the marshes to the south. The river is tidal at this point and when men and horses tried to cross they sank into the soft ooze. They reappeared the next day when the tide receded, making a macabre sight, dead yet still sitting erect on their horses, held upright by their saddles and armour. By the time Edward arrived back from what he had thought was part of a glorious victory de Montfort had won the battle and was besieging the last remnants of resistance in the castle. The casualties in this battle were quoted by the Abbot of St Pancras as 2,700 which probably represents those found and buried in and around the town. Several hundred more found other resting places. A reasonable estimate of the total would be four thousand, perhaps one out of every five engaged. However, the battlefield was in a confined area, being bounded by a town, a river, and a steep slope, and, once the fighting began, survival was more a matter of luck than of skill.

In the nineteenth century various burial pits were discovered by builders. Some were found in 1810 and others in 1846. On the latter occasion a railway was being made through the Priory. The bones were simply thrown into the embankment, a typical example of the material outlook of the age.

The battlefield as a whole is best seen today from the ramparts of Lewes castle, where there is an arrow pointing toward s it. The perfect death trap of the meadows may be clearly appreciated.

De Montfort's masterly handling of the battle is best realized by climbing the hill to his initial position. It is not possible to walk over the entire battlefield for Lewes gaol is on a part of it but a clear enough picture may be obtained from various viewpoints without ever leaving the roads. Whether de Montfort so shrewdly judged Prince Edward that he planned to remove him from the battlefield entirely by offering him an easy and tempting target will never be known, but it may have been so. Rash though Edward had been he was prepared to continue the fight when he returned, and make up for his impetuosity, but he was unable to rally adequate support at that late stage. It is said that if Edward had not fallen into de Montfort's tactical trap the latter could have achieved as good a result by setting fire to the town and then attacking from behind the royalist position. Finally, Henry, with his army dispersed, had no alternative but to surrender, and was kept under arrest for the next fifteen months.

It was a fierce, bloody, and interesting battle. As at Hastings the right wing of the more numerous army pushed ahead and won a temporary victory but by becoming separated from the main body weakened the total effort. At Hastings however the right wing suffered heavy casualties through pressing forward, which did not happen at Lewes. At Edgehill an over-enthusiastic charge took most of the royalist cavalry off the field of battle; when they returned it was too late for them to have any effect on a battle which had gone badly for their side.

The length of the battle is not known but in all probability it was over by midday. There have been a number of theories about it. One makes an even closer parallel with Hastings in that it suggests that de Montfort remained on the defensive at the top of the hill. This seems highly unlikely for Henry's army had nothing to gain and everything to lose by storming a hill position which the rebels could not live on for more than a day or two. There was no food to be found in that area and an army of several thousand could never afford to stay long in one position in the Middle Ages, unless local food supplies were exceptionally plentiful.

Apart from the battlefield and the castle (with an adjoining museum) it is also possible to visit the ruins of the Cluniac Priory of St Pancras, just south of the town. It was founded by William, the first Earl Warenne, whose coffin was dug up in the nineteenth century, and now lies in Southover Church. He was one of the most powerful of the Norman barons who came over with the Conqueror but although a fearsome man in battle was given to pious works when not wielding his sword.

As we have noted, the majority of the battle was probably fought close to the castle. De Montfort probably drew up his front between the Chalk Pits and the Racecourse grandstand. He had marched that night from Fletching and caught Henry's look-out on Offham asleep. Doubtless the sentry was persuaded in a medieval way to give as much assistance and information as he could to the rebel earl. De Montfort may have planned to let the king attack him in this strong position, and then perhaps use his reserve in an encircling movement but seeing Prince Edward disappear from the battlefield probably caused him to change his plan and to charge on to a much diminished and disorganized royal army. As in many medieval battles the general outline is well known but the details are obscure. The modern visitor may perhaps come as near to guessing the truth as the expert.

The peace terms after the Battle of Lewes were of considerable importance for they set the stage for the return match which would be at Evesham fifteen months later. They were known as the *Mise of Lewes* but unfortunately no written record of them survives. The gist of them was that Henry was bound to act on the advice of his counsellors and dismiss his foreign favourites and that Prince Edward, his son, and Prince Henry, his nephew, should be hostages for his good behaviour. The two princes apparently did not have too dull a time for they were moved from one castle to another, Dover, Berkhamsted and Wallingford being mentioned. At Wallingford there was a chance that they might be released by royalist supporters but this possibility was discouraged by Edward when he was told that any rescue attempt would merely cause him to be launched from the castle by siege catapult. Eventually he was sent to Kenilworth.

THE BATTLE OF EVESHAM
4 August 1265

In the year following Henry III's defeat at Lewes conditions in England deteriorated generally. Parts of the country were still royalist, and among them were the Cinque Ports, which was inconvenient for commerce. In the uncertain conditions lawlessness increased; it was illegal to bear arms without a licence but the law was often flouted. As trade flagged and prices rose there was a general restlessness through the country that operated against honest work and effort. There was also general uneasiness at the knowledge that the lawful monarch was under continuous arrest, and that his son was in confinement as a hostage. However irritating Henry may have been as a monarch it seemed quite wrong that he should be dragged around the country as a prisoner. There was discontent with de Montfort for other reasons too; he was pious but his supporters felt that he had gained too much from military success, and they themselves too little. High-minded people are especially irritating when their lofty principles cause them to withhold rewards from others if at the same time they confer substantial benefits on themselves. There were doubtless good military reasons for his acquiring eighteen confiscated baronies, and the royal castles which had been captured, but they were not apparent to those less well-rewarded. By the spring of 1265 he had alienated such powerful supporters as Gilbert de Clare, Earl of Gloucester, and Roger Mortimer. A strong opposition began to build up m the west country and was soon joined by barons who had fled overseas after their defeat at Lewes; among them were John de Warenne, of Surrey, and William de Valence, Earl of Pembroke. De Montfort set off to Hereford to crush this growing threat. But the danger was much more widespread than he realized at first. An army was being mustered in Pembrokeshire, there was incipient rebellion in Worcestershire, and royalist supporters were bearing arms openly and defiantly in the north. De Montfort may have been haughty and overbearing but he was no fool and knew when flexibility was the best policy. He promptly sent a letter to the King of France requesting him to act as arbitrator and reconciler between himself and his discontented supporters. If it gained nothing else it would gain time for his opponents to begin quarrelling among themselves. Unfortunately for this astute appreciation Prince Edward managed to escape at the end of that month while on a little hunting party he had persuaded his guardians to arrange, while confined at Hereford. He soon outstripped the rest of the hunt and reached safety at Wigmore castle (the main stronghold of the Mortimers).

After this there was no chance of reconciliation. De Montfort still had the king in custody and claimed that he was ruling with royal consent, but this in no way impeded Prince Edward from strengthening his position by taking in the north-western counties. De Montfort, who was a man of action as much as a diplomat, moved through Gloucester to Wales where he tried to make an effective alliance with Llewellyn. His journey into Wales was not a success and he retired to Newport waiting for supplies and reinforcements. He was disappointed. The supply fleet was engaged and wrecked by the royalists. There was no point in remaining. With a greatly dispirited army de Montfort moved north again to Hereford. It was not a pleasant journey, but it was a very necessary one, for de Clare and Prince Edward were now on the Severn and it was essential to move quickly if he was to get back across again. He had sent instructions to his son Simon to collect an army and take it up to Kenilworth, which was the principal de Montfort castle. Simon de Montfort the Younger took unduly long over his task but for all the good he did on arrival he might just as well have taken longer. On arrival at Kenilworth, which was a very strong castle surrounded by III acres of water he very unwisely quartered his army in the town instead of the castle. Prince Edward, who was an early pioneer of army intelligence, knew all about de Montfort the Younger and the movements of his army. Acting on the knowledge his spies and scouts brought him he made a forced night march and caught the rebel army just before dawn. The surprise was so complete that there was virtually no resistance and young de Montfort himself escaped naked into the castle. This was 1 August.

During the previous weeks de Montfort had been looking for a place where he could cross the Severn. Knowing that the rebel earl needed to do this urgently and return to England at the earliest opportunity Prince Edward and his allies had destroyed all the bridges and deepened all possible fords. Furthermore, they had kept careful watch along the eastern bank; some of the watching had been done by the earl's discontented former supporters. However, at last de Montfort found an unguarded crossing place at Kempsey, four miles south of Worcester. Once across, he planned to march straight to Kenilworth and join up with his son's forces, but to do so he needed to keep well clear of Worcester, which was in royalist hands. Accordingly he took the Pershore road to Evesham, a distance of fifteen miles; at the latter he would turn north to Warwick and Kenilworth. Both armies were now very weary, de Montfort after scanty feeding in Wales and a night crossing followed by a swift march, Prince Edward after a forced march, a lightning victory, and a swift counter-march. Although knowing he would now get no support from his son, Edward was determined that de Montfort should not reach the safe haven of the castle, where he could reconstruct his plans at leisure. Although utterly weary, the prince put his army on the road again to head the earl off his objective.

It was a masterly and decisive move, fully worthy of the great strategist the young Edward would become later. To block every path open to de Montfort, he took the risk in dividing his force, and split it into three 'battles'; he commanded one himself, gave one to de Clare, Earl of Gloucester (who had fought valiantly for de Montfort at Lewes) and the other to Mortimer . He himself came from due north, Gloucester from the north-west, and Mortimer from due west.

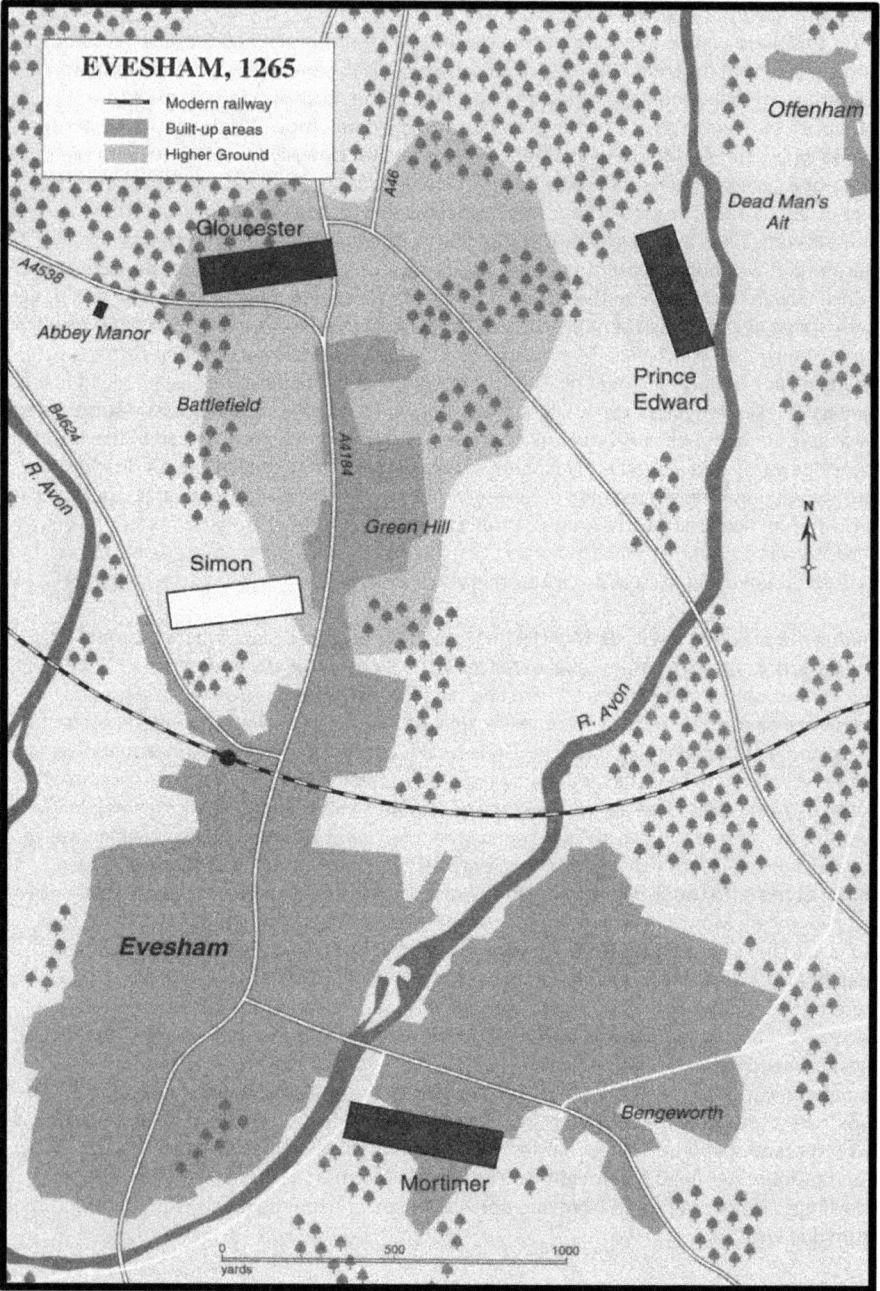

EVESHAM, 1265

- Modern railway
- Built-up areas
- Higher Ground

Offenham

Gloucester

A46

A4538

Dead Man's Ait

Abbey Manor

B4624

Battlefield

A4184

R. Avon

Prince Edward

N

Green Hill

Simon

R. Avon

Evesham

Bengeworth

Mortimer

0   500   1000
yards

There is a memorial obelisk in the grounds of the Abbey Manor. The battle took place on the slopes below 'Dead Man's Ait', the meadow where most of the slaughter took place, is opposite the Bridge Inn (known as The Boat) at Offenham (Worcestershire)

The key to the disaster which then overtook de Montfort is the situation of Evesham. At this point there is a loop in the river Avon, and Evesham lies at the southern end of it. On the morning of 4 August de Montfort had reached the abbey and was resting there, possibly in consideration of his royal burden, who at the age of fifty- seven was probably feeling and showing the effects of the long marches and privations. He did not know exactly where Prince Edward was and would not suspect that his son's army had been already destroyed. He might have hoped that the young man would send out a supporting force down the road from Kenilworth and might appear from the north, or east over Offenham bridge (which no longer exists). When he heard that a large army was moving down from the north he believed that this was what was happening, particularly as a look-out reported seeing de Montfort banners in the van; he was correct, they were banners captured by Prince Edward at Kenilworth. Soon, however, the look-out saw less welcome sights, Prince Edward's banner following close behind the captured standards and far worse still, Gloucester banners were to be seen on the road from the north-west, and Mortimer banners to the south - behind him. Had he wished he could still have escaped on a fast horse over the bridge but his army was doomed and he knew it. The only words of despair he uttered were 'Now God have mercy on our souls, for our bodies are theirs.' He urged others to leave, among them Philip Basset, who had done so much for his cause, but no one would desert him.

As the enemy approached, the old earl marshalled his army in battle array, and with himself at its head launched it at Prince Edward's advancing army. If by some wild stroke of luck he could kill the young prince he might - it was a very slender chance - so discomfort his opponents that they would come to terms. He nearly succeeded, for he hit them with such a shock that they had to be steadied by Warine of Bassingbourn. Already outnumbered by three to one de Montfort's army took another shock when Gloucester's army came on to their flanks and rear. But they fought on. The only supporters they had lost were Welsh archers who had already begun to slip away as he marched to meet Prince Edward's army; they failed to escape and were mostly killed on Dead Man's Ait (or Eyot), another bloody meadow just opposite the Bridge Inn at Offenham. The battle degenerated into slaughter, and the chronicler (Robert of Gloucester) recorded it as 'the murder of Evesham for battle it was not'. De Montfort, who had his horse killed beneath him, and saw his son being killed next to him, grasped his sword with both hands and tried to hack a path into the centre of the royalist force. He fell under a dozen strokes. So great was the hatred that had been aroused that his body was mutilated and his head stuck on a pole. In the heat of the fighting the captive Henry was knocked to the ground and nearly killed, being thought to be a de Montfort supporter. It is said that he only saved his life by calling out: 'Do not kill me, I am Henry of Winchester, your king.'

In spite of this crushing victory the war dragged on for a further two years in desultory sieges.

The battlefield is badly marked and difficult to access. Above the slopes on which the battle was fought is a monument hidden in the trees but approachable by a footpath from the road. It bears the inscription: *On this spot in the reign of Henry III the Battle of Evesham was fought August I V, 1265 between the King 's forces commanded by his eldest son Prince Edward and the Barons under Simon de Montfort, Earl of Leicester, in which the Prince, by his skilled valour, obtained a complete victory. The Earl with his eldest son, Henry of Montfort, eighteen barons, one hundred and sixty knights and four thousand soldiers were slain in the battle.*

The battle itself was fought in a thunderstorm, and at times the field was so dark men could scarcely distinguish friend from foe. Montfort's remains, or what could be found of them, were buried in Evesham Abbey. His tomb became a place of pilgrimage and it was said that many people were cured of ailments by praying there. The abbey and tomb were destroyed in the reign of Henry VIII.

The obelisk, which was erected in 1845, is said to mark the spot where de Montfort was killed but this is unlikely; it was probably put in that conspicuous position to enable visitors to survey the battlefield from the best vantage point. Nowadays the obelisk is completely obscured by trees, although it can still be reached by an overgrown path. 'Dead Man's Ait', where the Welsh and many others were slaughtered, may be reached by ferry from the Bridge Inn at Offenham. The inn is known locally as 'The Boat'. Up till two hundred years ago there was a narrow stone bridge there and a usable ford.

The wholesale and merciless slaughter at Evesham was partly in revenge for Lewes. Welsh archers were probably employed by both sides and would have no compunction about slaughtering each other for there was bitterer hatred and rivalry in Wales than anywhere else in the British Isles. All guerrilla fighters have a hard time when they are eventually trapped by their opponents.

The main battle is said to have lasted less than two hours, but the hunting of fugitives doubtless went on all day.

THE BATTLE OF PILLETH
22 June 1402

After the Battle of Evesham there were no other disturbances in Henry III's reign. Towards the end of it Prince Edward went off on a crusade, where he distinguished himself, as might have been expected. In 1272 when Henry died he succeeded and England was ruled for the next thirty-five years by her most able warrior-king, now known as Edward I. His greatest memorial is probably the great castles he built in Wales: Harlech, Conway, Caernarvon, and Beaumaris are excellent examples. He was equally forceful in Scotland and France.

When Edward I died his son Edward II proved to be completely unlike him. Though idle, irresponsible, and cowardly, he lasted for twenty years before being murdered at Berkeley Castle. His son Edward III who followed him to the throne was the complete opposite, and much like his grandfather Edward I. He was only fourteen when he succeeded but by the end of his fifty-year reign he had won battle after battle, notable among them being Halidon Hill (1333), Crecy (1346) and Poitiers (1356). His son was the famous Black Prince but the latter had died before him, and the throne went to the Black Prince's son, Richard II. Richard II came to the throne at the age of ten and reigned for two more years than his notorious grandfather Edward II, whom in many ways he resembled. It is, of course, unwise to be too critical of events which happened so long ago, and there may be more in Richard's favour than history has so far brought to light. But the general verdict is that his reign was a wretched and unsuccessful tyranny, which was only brought to an end when the throne was usurped by his cousin Henry of Boling- broke, whom he had treated unwisely and perhaps unjustly. There was no battle involved. Richard's supporters fell away, and his cousin had no difficulty in taking the crown. How Richard's life ended is not known. He was sent to Pontefract castle and no story ever emerged to tell of his fate, although he was certainly murdered. The secret was well-kept. The new king, who became Henry IV, had a difficult reign of fourteen years, before he died of leprosy. Needless to say there were plenty of his subjects who were shocked by the fate, unknown but suspected, of Richard II, and plenty more who were prepared to pretend they were if they could turn the circumstances to their own advantage. Civil war broke out within two months of his accession but he was quick to act and some vigorous head-chopping stabilized his position again. But this was a domestic matter and did not involve more than a few discontented and badly-organized earls. A rebellion which broke out in 1400 was a far more serious affair. Owen-ap-Griffith (ap =son of) of Glendower had been one of Richard's squires and had a respect and liking for him. He was also a genius at guerrilla warfare. As a descendant of Prince Llewellyn, of Welsh royal blood, he could claim that he was ruling Wales by appointment from Richard II whom he claimed was still alive but living in exile in Scotland. Glendower captured a number of English-held castles in Wales, though some defeated him; and he made nonsense of Henry IV's attempts to apprehend him. He proclaimed himself Prince of North Wales, and there was nobody who could deny his de facto right to the title.

The task of suppressing him was given to Edmund Mortimer who came of a family with generations of border fighting experience. As he was closely related to Richard n it may seem surprising that he should be assisting his murderer but the explanation is that he and his tenants felt they might lose their lives and property in the next raid if Glendower was not checked. Glendower had recently be- headed the entire garrison, sixty men in all, of New Radnor castle when he had captured it; he buried heads and bodies separately. Mortimer, therefore, had little difficulty in raising an army from people who were tired of having their property plundered by raiders from Wales, and from others who thought a little Welsh rape and pillage would be most acceptable, and set off to teach Glendower a lesson. The people in these areas had fought each other so often that there was virtually a D.S.(1) solution to every problem. In this situation experience had taught invaders that it was unwise to move up the valley which was marshy and difficult; a sudden attack might send the entire column floundering into a morass. Just beyond Whitton the invaders came to Pilleth where many years before the Normans had built a motte and bailey castle blocking the valley; the wooden ramparts and tower have long since disappeared but the formidable earthworks remain. Further along the valley are tumuli which tell of more ancient wars.

(1) D.S. Directing staff. The D.S. solution is the Instructor's view. The Instructors at Staff Colleges and military training establishments are known as the Directing Staff.

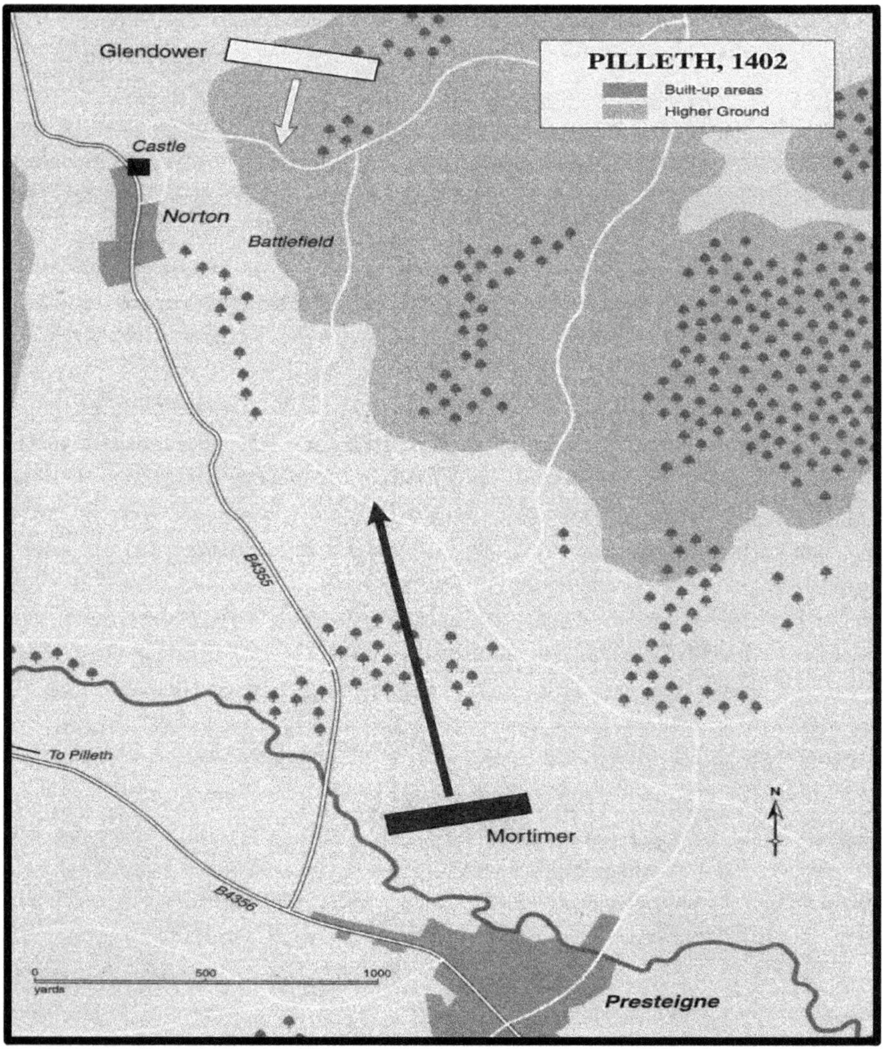

PILLETH, 1402

Built-up areas
Higher Ground

Glendower

Castle

Norton

Battlefield

B4355

To Pilleth

B4356

Mortimer

0   500   1000
yards

N

Presteigne

Take the road from Presteigne, and Pilleth will be found just past Whitton. The battle site may be seen clearly from the road. (Powys)

Mortimer was not going to be caught in the marsh like many of his predecessors had been. He therefore kept well to the right and moved on to a spur, which was separated by another valley from the next ridge. It was the sort of choice you had to take in war, risky and unpleasant because the lower part of the hill was covered with bracken and the upper part with gorse but it was the sort of gamble they had taken a dozen times before, and been none the worse for it. But on this occasion they were up against the astute military brain of one of the greatest of guerrilla fighters, Owen Glendower. Colonel Topham Hood, who as the tenant of the battlefield had plenty of time to reconstruct the events, considers that Glendower must have been watching Mortimer all the time he advanced up the valley. At the top of the ridge Glendower was in a perfect position to observe his enemy advance, then launch a frontal attack down the steep slope or - if Mortimer persisted in keeping to the valley - come in on his flanks just where he was threading his way through the marsh.

Doubtless Mortimer sent scouts up the slope to make sure all was well. They did not report any unusual occurrence, which is not surprising, for they would all be lying with their throats cut in the bracken where they had been swiftly and silently ambushed.

Halfway up the hill Mortimer realized his terrible mistake. The Welsh poured on to his army, first smothering them with arrows, then bearing down the hill in what seemed an endless rush. The slope is like the roof of a house and as the English forced tired men and horses up it the Welsh hurled them or their corpses down again. Mortimer was singled out to be taken prisoner but others were not so lucky. The Welsh were too excited to give much thought to the possibilities of ransoms, and the fighting was altogether too fierce and bloody for nice considerations of rank and precedence. Today in the middle of that field is a grove of trees which were planted on a pit of bones. Perhaps the pit did not need to be dug but was a natural hollow which filled up as men encountered it unawares. According to local report the Welsh camp followers of Glendower shamelessly mutilated the corpses of the dead English; perhaps it seemed an appropriate revenge for the treatment they had often received from invaders for their principal activity was castration. No one troubled to bury the dead for a long time and the reek of the hillside of decaying corpses caused the area to be shunned for months. The hill was called Bryn Glas, and the battle is sometimes known by that name.

All that needs to be seen of the battlefield may be seen from the road which approaches it and runs alongside. The hillside is now bare of gorse and bracken, and is covered with close-cropped turf. The little churchyard where some of the most important personages were buried has no record of them.

The battlefield was doubtless plundered immediately afterwards, before the corpses began to rot; the only relic which was subsequently discovered was a pair of revolving spurs, wicked enough but not unique.

Among the many killed that day was Sir Walter Devereux of Weobley, and Sir Robert Whitney, who was Knight-Marshal to Henry IV.

Mortimer, very soon afterwards, married Glendower's daughter, and announced to his own followers that he was now in alliance with the latter to restore the rightful line to the English throne. The rightful line was his own nephew, the Earl of March, who certainly had a better claim that Henry IV, but as a mere boy could only be the pawn of greedy and power-seeking barons. It is said that Henry had refused to ransom Mortimer. Subsequently, when Glendower's army had been scattered Mortimer died at Harlech castle which was then under siege (1409).

THE BATTLE OF SHREWSBURY
21 July 1403

After Pilleth there was little that Henry IV could do to restrain the Welsh for he had too many other troubles on his hands. Norman privateers crossed the Channel and raided the south coast, Scots under the redoubtable Douglas crossed the border and harried the northern counties. At Homildon Hill, on 14 September 1402, two miles west of Wooler, he mustered a reputed 10,000 Scots. On the English side, inevitably, was the chief enemy of the Scots, Earl Percy, of Northumberland. It was a victory for the English archers, for the longbow so outdistanced the Scottish short bow that the Scots were nearly annihilated before they could get to close quarters. When they did the odds were in favour of the English who completed the carnage with charges. Always in the forefront of the battle was Harry Percy, the Earl's son, who was known as Hotspur from his activities in the forefront of battle. Among the Scottish prisoners they took on that day were Murdoch of Albany, Earl Douglas, Earl Moray and Earl Orkney. The ransoms of these powerful noblemen were worth a fortune. To the disgust of the victors they were required by Henry IV to hand over the prisoners so that he could use their ransoms to bolster his own sagging finances. Earl Percy took it very badly for he had previously been Henry's main support and felt that at the very least he should be allowed to profit from his own successes. Henry would not hear a word of it. Rewards would come from him later, if and when he chose. It was not a very intelligent message to send to a border chieftain flushed with victory and power. Northumberland's reaction was entirely predictable; he decided that Henry IV had become unreasonable, and should be dethroned at the earliest possible moment . To that end he began negotiations with Glendower, who in turn brought in the French. Northumberland also released Douglas who rallied a Scottish force. The plan was that after having deposed Henry they would install the Earl of March (cousin of the Mortimer captured at Pilleth) who was next in line to the throne, in his place, while dividing the kingdom between them. By July 1403 they felt ready to act. On the ninth Hotspur marched into Cheshire by the side of his traditional enemy, Earl Douglas. From Cheshire after brisk recruiting he moved to Stafford, where he was joined by his uncle, the Earl of Worcester; all three then set off to Shrewsbury where they had arranged to meet Glendower with a substantial force from Wales. To do so he needed to reach the town before Henry IV, as whoever held Shrewsbury commanded the passage of the Severn at that point. Once the alarm was given in medieval warfare the rival armies raced to the vital nodal point, knowing that 'history repeats itself because geography remains a constant'. Henry reached the town on the night of the twentieth; Hotspur reached it on the Saturday morning. The key to the king's success seems to be that he had marched from Lichfield in a day - a distance of forty-one miles. Hotspur could probably have made the effort and beaten him if he had realized the urgent necessity of the task although he had already marched nearly 250 miles but he did not and the rebels' fate was thereby sealed. When Hotspur arrived he found the gates locked and Henry's banners on display; this was ominous because Henry's army was considerably larger than the rebels'.

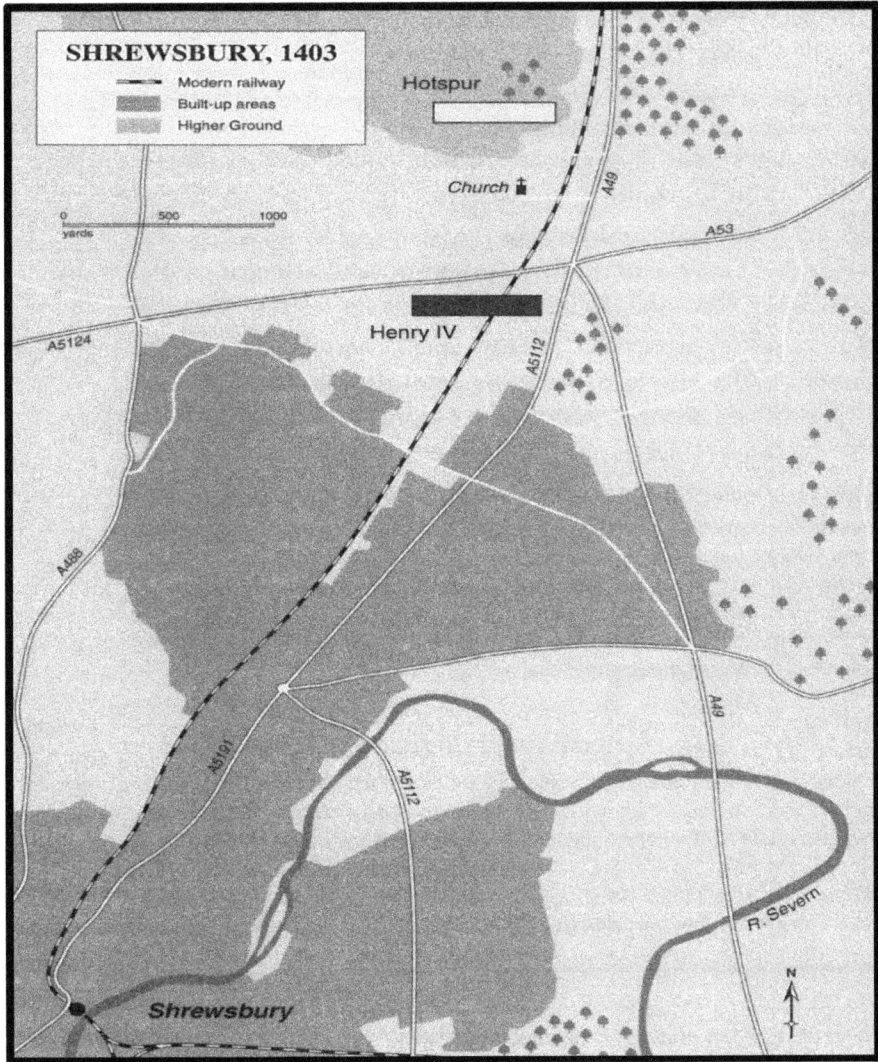

SHREWSBURY, 1403

- ===== Modern railway
- ▓▓ Built-up areas
- ░░ Higher Ground

0   500   1000
yards

Hotspur

Church

A49

A53

Henry IV

A5124

A5112

A488

A5191

A5112

A49

R. Severn

Shrewsbury

N

The battlefield lies just off the A49 road three miles out of Shrewsbury (Shropshire).

There was no sign of Glendower who was reputed to be on the way from Oswestry. According to his own story he had been delayed by floods and had made the best haste he could; according to his critics he had dawdled along and then watched the inevitable battle from a convenient tree at Shelton, a mile or so away, prior to declaring his allegiance to either party; the latter view was somewhat unfair to a great guerrilla leader, although it must be admitted that for him to be on the losing side would be as disastrous for his country as himself, and whatever else the Welsh might be accused of it could never be lack of courage. In fact Glendower was still in Carmarthen. Denied entrance to the city, and short of expected numbers, Hotspur fell back and took up position on a site he had surveyed the day before. He knew that Henry must come out and attempt to destroy him, for in medieval warfare when the time to give battle came it must be taken or your own side might accuse you of cowardice and melt away to join the opposition. Hotspur's position was on a slope about three miles along the Whitchurch road. He probably felt that it was good enough for his purpose but if he had known the country a little better he could have taken up a greatly superior position two miles to the south-east on Haughmond Hill. However, it is not possible to be dogmatic about the choice of medieval battlefields. Low ground could be marshier; high ground could be more difficult to access. For his purpose the area known as 'Battlefield' was entirely adequate. Hotspur, who was thirty-nine and by no means the hot-headed youth depicted in Shakespeare, had won many a battle and had every intention of winning this one. He required a ridge from which his bowmen could survey the advancing army, and a few hazards at the bottom of the slope. The battlefield has probably not altered very much since his day, although now there is a church in the middle of it. One of the best places to survey it is from the bridge over the railway line. Hotspur seems to have positioned his army along the ridge behind the old track through Allbright Hussey. On his immediate front there was a field of peas, and ahead of that were ponds. As the enemy funneled past the ponds and advanced with difficulty through the tangle of fully grown peas they would make useful targets for the bowmen he had recently recruited in Cheshire. This was the great age of the archer. Nearly sixty years before they had cut the French to pieces at Crecy; now two well-matched armies - the smaller with an advantage of ground - were going to fight one of the greatest of all longbow battles.

The longbow, which both sides would be using with deadly effect, was reasonably accurate at 240 yards. At shorter distance it could be as deadly as a rifle; at longer ranges, particularly if aided by wind or slope it could blanket a target like a creeping artillery barrage. A trained archer- which means a man who could send off up to a dozen arrows a minute- was an invaluable asset but he had to be kept at fighting pitch by constant practice. The bow had a seventy- pound pull, and there was considerable skill in reloading at speed. Five thousand archers averaging a mere ten shots a minute could cover the target with arrows coming from every level. They would have a devastating effect on horses and their riders, however well-armoured both might be. In the twelfth century there was a revealing story of a knight who was caught by an arrow which went through his mailed skirt, his leg, his saddle, and into the horse. He turned to ride out of battle and have it attended to, and as he did another arrow did exactly the same for the other leg. It was recounted not because of the power of the arrow but because it was an unusual occurrence like a man having a rifle bullet pass right through his chest without touching a vital organ. That first shower of arrows was something you merely hoped to live through; if it missed you, you would be on to the archers to cut them to pieces before they could recover or obtain fresh supplies. But if the shock sent your army staggering those same archers would be among you with hammers to crack open your armour and long daggers to push through the cracks. A medieval battle might sometimes be delayed by parleying - as on this occasion - but once the first arrows sped away there was no drawing back.

The ponds which are mentioned in some accounts, but which can no longer be seen, were perhaps marshy patches, but probably something much deeper. The disappearance of any holes on a battlefield is easily explained; the casualties from both sides were rolled in and earth thrown on top. Who would dig a hole big enough for a mass grave if he could roll the corpses into something put there by nature; in all probability it would be half full of corpses already.

It seems that on this occasion Hotspur's bowmen may have been deceived over the dispositions of the advancing royal army, which had probably fanned out more than expected. Prince Henry (later Henry V) commanded the left wing while the king commanded the right. Neither seems to have received the full benefit of the opening archery volleys, which must have concentrated on the centre, for both were able to put in powerful attacks making a pincer movement by oblique approaches into the rebel centre. As Hotspur's army was drawn up in line, and would be in three battles, the pincers would close at the divisions, and, as every soldier knows, there is no better position to put in pressure. If the battles, regiments, or combat teams have never fought together before, and if they come from different parts of the country - or even different countries - there is remarkable confusion, probably misdirected effort, and a feeling that others are letting you down. In times like that, good leaders rally their men and try to get them moving forward .This is what Hotspur and Douglas did. They knew by long experience that at this point in the battle victory hung in the balance and depended on morale. With spearmen, archers, and cavalrymen milling around in a tangle of personal combats the only way was to drive a path through the confusion and kill someone important on the other side. Prince Henry had already received an arrow in his face, which had sent him to the rear, so it was the king or nothing. In the event it was nothing, for Hotspur received a fatal jab in the general press, and when he fell the rebel spirit began to crumble. The rebel army fell back on to higher ground but there was no one capable of rallying them and turning defeat into victory. Back they went, and finally broke and fled. Douglas, seeing all was lost, decided to leave and fight another day. He broke from the fight, spurred his horse towards Haughmond where he could have obtained sanctuary in the abbey but fell before he reached it, and lay on the ground with a broken knee-cap. But he was much too valuable as a potential ally to be killed. He was given treatment and then set free by the king. Others were less lucky. Worcester and most of the other rebel leaders were beheaded, and Worcester's head had the honour of being impaled on a spike on London Bridge.

Hotspur's corpse had even more humiliating treatment. It was buried honourably, then exhumed, displayed in Shrewsbury and finally quartered. In the medieval custom a limb was sent to each town from which he had drawn support.

Most of the fighting settled down to the point on which the church now stands. It is said to be built on a pit of bones but bones do not make the most secure foundation and it probably stands alongside the biggest burial pit. It was not built by a grateful King Henry IV but by a neighbouring rector (Roger Ive, of Allbrighton Hussey) on a site given by Richard Hussey in 1406. The place now known as Battlefield was then Haytelfeld. The original name of a battlefield often helps to tell us more than all contemporary accounts for it often gives us the reason why events occurred as they did. Here there is a choice. Haytelfeld may have derived its name from 'hay' meaning grass of the variety which would grow long in a marshy area, or from 'haies' the old Norman hedges which could afford shelter or cover. The ground today is not too difficult, although there is a sunken road which could have been a death-trap - or perfect cover - and some sudden changes of level which would play havoc with a charge.

A disconcerting feature of this battle was that Henry IV took the precaution of having several of his retainers dressed as royalty while he himself wore inconspicuous clothing. Doubtless he had no difficulty in obtaining 'volunteers' for this dangerous task. It was a sound plan economically for most of them were probably killed and did not need to be paid - let alone rewarded. And it was very disconcerting for the rebels. Deception did not occur often in medieval warfare but here was used with considerable success. Few things can have been more frustrating than to reach your chief opponent only to discover it is not him after all as the real man is, apparently, two dozen yards away.

The numbers on the battlefield are not precisely known but it seems probable that there were 14,000 on the king's side and about 11,000 on the rebels'. Estimates of 20,000 a side are obviously too high, for such numbers could never have found a space on the battlefield. Even the smaller, more feasible figure was probably not committed all at once. It is thought the duration of the battle was four hours but the aftermath would go on most of the day. The battlefield is easy to find, and survey. The church was long since robbed of its commemorative glass but has the coats of arms of the victors inside; gargoyles, which are supposed to represent the rebels, are on the gutters outside. The gargoyles are lifelike and were probably recognizable likenesses.

Although the result was doubtless regarded with mixed feelings by many, it left the country in a more stable position than if the rebels had won. Militarily it was a triumph for the better tactician, and in view of the experience and power of the rebels was a remarkable achievement. Henry IV was probably one of the greatest of the warrior kings. If he had ever been able to set out on a path of foreign conquest his successes could have been dazzling. After the battle Henry's army moved west and confronted Glendower's at Leominster. Glendower summed up the situation, decided there was no gain to be made from a fixed battle, and slipped back into Wales. Henry was too wise to follow on that occasion.

After winning the battle of Shrewsbury Henry had only a temporary lull before other troubles came his way. The source of most of them was Hotspur's father, the Earl of Northumberland. In 1405 he managed to stimulate another rebellion, in which the Earl of Nottingham and the Archbishop of York were leading figures. However, these two were duped into coming to a conference with the royal commander (the Earl of Westmorland), arrested, and executed. Northumberland had been too wily to come to the conference but had to make a quick departure and hide away in Scotland for two years. Two years later he was back and making a quick drive on York. Unfortunately for his plans he was caught at Bramham Moor where he put up a tremendous fight before being killed; he was seventy. Two years later, Henry met another trouble, and one which he could not shake off. It was leprosy, and in 1413 he died of it. England was lucky in that neither Scotland nor France were in a position to give much trouble at this time. When his son Henry v came to the throne he was permanently on the offensive and in his nine years reign won his battles with devastating ease. His first great triumph was Agincourt in 1415, and from this he went on to conquer most of northern France. The French were assisted by Scottish troops but it made no difference to the result. Henry died in the hour of his triumph, in 1422, at the age of thirty-four. His successor Henry VI soon managed to lose all the French conquests of the previous reign, and through no fault of his own, plunged England into suicidal wars which lasted for thirty years.

The key to the tangle of battles which are known as the Wars of the Roses was the usurpation of the English throne by Henry IV. As we saw in the previous chapter, Henry IV never succeeded in enjoying the throne he had gained by murdering his cousin Richard n, and subsequently Henry V's path of conquest so occupied men's minds that they had little time to reflect on whether the true heir sat on the throne or not. When Henry v died it was a different story. His son was under a year old on his succession. That in itself was not too serious for he had an able guardian for his early years: this was the Duke of Bedford. However, the good effect of Bedford was largely offset by the follies of the Duke of Gloucester which largely contributed to the loss of France. An even greater contribution to disaster was made by the Duke of Somerset, but unfortunately Henry VI favoured him and made him his counsellor. A far more suitable choice was the Duke of York, but both Henry and his French wife, Queen Margaret, suspected (wrongly) that the duke might have designs on the crown, as he was a closer relative of the murdered King Richard than Henry himself was. York became the head of what became known as the Yorkist faction in the ensuing wars. Their badge was the White Rose and they numbered among their supporters the enormously wealthy and powerful younger branch of the Nevilles (the Earls of Salisbury and Warwick; the latter who changed sides later became known as the 'Kingmaker'). The younger Nevilles hated and opposed their cousins, the family of the Earl of Westmorland. All had the advantage of hosts of experienced soldiers who had fought in the French wars and these supporters often proved so obstreperous and turbulent that it was necessary to keep them employed before they found some private objective of their own to fight for. Supporting Henry VI were the Lancastrians- the party of the Red Rose (although the badge was not assumed at first) and they included such powerful and aggressive noblemen as the Duke of Somerset, the Percys of Northumberland, and the Staffords of Buckingham. How venomously the protagonists hated each other will be seen in the aftermath of the battles we shall describe. In one sense the war was regional, for the north, the west, and Wales adhered to the king while the Midlands, south, and east were Yorkist. Much blood would be spilt before this conflict would be resolved, and the end only came when most of the leaders of either side had been killed off. On the few occasions when it seemed that the bitter blood feuds might calm down, Henry went mad. However, the madder and more hopeless Henry became, the more relentlessly ferocious his Queen Margaret became.

The first battle took place not because Henry went mad but because, after eighteen months of insanity, he became sane again. While he was mad two interesting events had occurred. One was that York became Protector and ran the country to everyone's satisfaction - except the hard-core Lancastrians, the other was that Queen Margaret gave birth to a son after nine years of unsuccessful matrimony. It was suggested that Henry had had his husbandly efforts supplemented during the period of his madness but this was never proved, and the heir was regarded as legitimate. However, when Henry recovered, and at the instigation of the young mother dismissed York from his post, while restoring the hated and incompetent Somerset, the stage was set for the first battle.

York was not normally an impatient man but this was a little too much for him: he gathered his army of some 3,000 battle-experienced supporters and set off for London. He had no ambition to secure the throne but he was not prepared to see Somerset run and ruin the country, so he had prepared to see Somerset run and ruin the country, so he had prepared an ultimatum demanding that the latter should be tried. His move took Henry and his friends by surprise but they managed to muster an army of about 2,000 to intercept York at St Albans. St Albans is one of those few towns which has not so far been replaced with grim concrete blocks and the visitor today can still trace the battle. (There were in fact two battles of St Albans, the second taking place in 1461 when the Lancastrians won. By that time there had been many other bloody encounters.)

The First Battle of St Albans had an indecisive beginning but once it began was ferocious enough to satisfy the most bloodthirsty. York had hastened down from Yorkshire, knowing that he had supporters in the capital and that the nearer he got the better it was. Henry on the other hand wished to fight as far from London as possible. They met at St Albans which is twenty-one miles from London and on the top of a hill. Henry arrived first and was able to throw up a few barricades; York arrived on the eastern outskirts at approximately the same time, that is 7a.m. But instead of pushing on to defeat the smaller army before it could receive reinforcements, York waited. Reinforcements were not in fact available but York would not have cared greatly if they had been, for his aim was not so much to defeat the king in battle as to demonstrate that his policy was provoking determined opposition. For three hours the armies waited while a few vague messages passed back and forth. Finally York stated his terms as bluntly as he felt diplomatic; he required that the Duke of Somerset should be handed over to be executed.

Henry would have none of it. The battle was now inevitable.

Its course is easy to trace. Henry held the middle of the town with his H.Q in St Peter's Street, almost opposite the National Westminster Bank, which was the site of the old Castle Inn. The Yorkists left their halting place (Key Field) and moved in two columns up Sopwell Lane (halfway down the hill) and Victoria Street (this was then called Shropshire Lane). Both these were barricaded close to the point at which they emerged into St Peter's Street and Holywell Hill. At the other end of these roads was the Town Ditch, which was not as well defended as it should have been. The Yorkists had little difficulty in crossing the ditch which was thinly defended, partly because it was 1,000 yards long and partly because some of its defenders had left their posts during the parley, under the impression that there would be no fighting to do. When battle began the dispositions along the line were not good enough to stop determined threats by the Yorkists. In the streets, by the barricade, it was a different story and it looked as if the struggle would be long-drawn, if not entirely inconclusive.

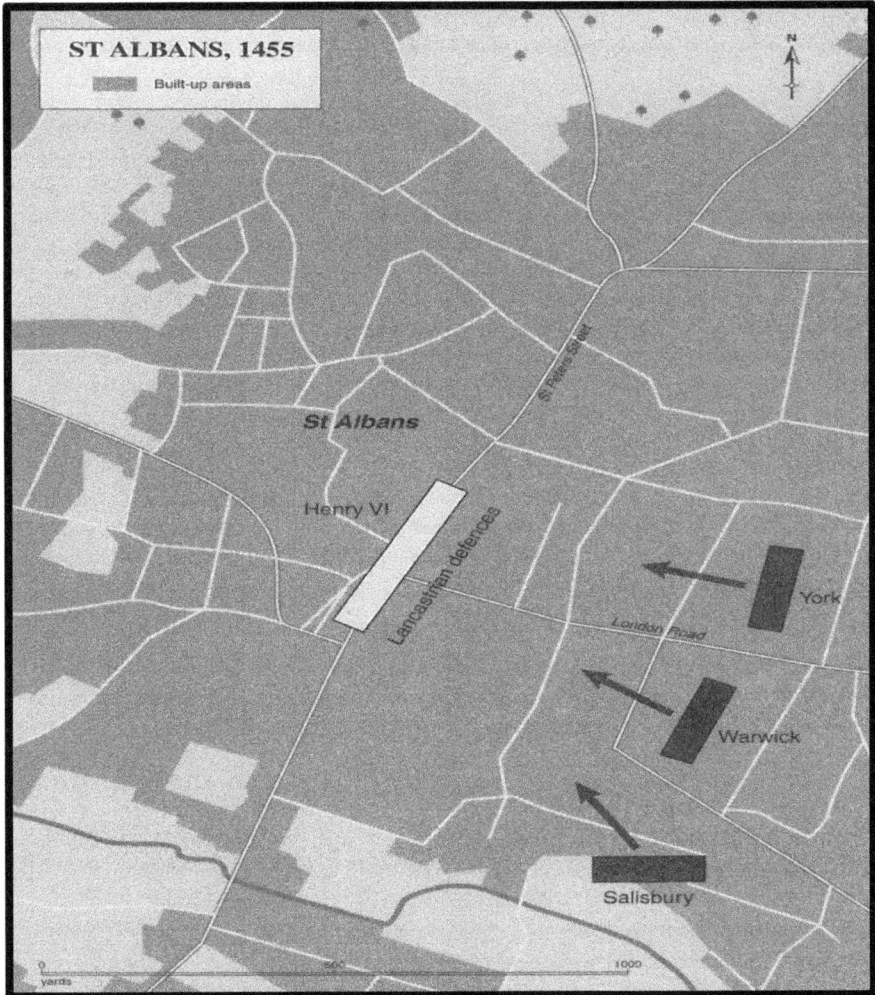

The best way to see the battle site is to start in St Peter's Street; most of the roads retain their fifteenth century alignment, as indeed many of the buildings retain their characters. (Hertfordshire)

The deadlock was broken by Warwick, who gave a taste of the drive he would later show in other battles. He was already twenty- five so the popular story that he was little more than a headstrong boy belongs to romance not reality. The route he took is over the London road.

Warwick took a look at the houses on the inner side of the ditch and decided he could get through them. These, and all the other buildings which backed onto the ditch were known as the 'Town Backsides'. He crossed the ditch and began to batter a way through the not very substantial medieval walls. Probably the royal forces were too occupied with street fighting to be alert to what was happening, for their first intimation of his activities was when he broke through the walls of an old house into St Peter's Street right in the middle of the Lancastrian position. The rest of the Yorkists were quick to follow and in minutes the roadway was full of men hacking, stabbing, and slashing at each other. Those behind loosed off arrows into the tightly packed opposition. The slaughter was concentrated, and contemporary accounts leave none of the details to the imagination. Henry himself was wounded by an arrow and might well have been killed in the general excitement had he not been taken away to a tanner's cottage. The battle lasted half an hour only, but inevitably St Albans suffered from the exuberance of the victors *after* the conflict. Somerset was killed in the battle so, with his war aims achieved, York was able to come to Henry - in the tanner's cottage, go down on his knees, and beg forgiveness. Henry granted it.

It is said that the principal casualties were all among the nobility; it seems improbable. Undoubtedly noblemen were killed but it is naive to accept the frequently made assertion that the higher ranks were singled out and the remainder were left untouched. What is more likely is that the slaughter was heavy enough among the men-at-arms but on this occasion the knights in armour had to fight dismounted, were in the thick of it with no avenue of escape, and were not spared for their ransom value. However, it was reported that not more than a hundred were killed. In the press it would be difficult to do more than lunge, hack and stab at heads and shoulders. It would look spectacular enough from the roofs of the nearby buildings but could not, in the circumstances, have been as murderous as battles in which there was more room for action.

Medieval battles had different types of casualties from modern warfare. Then, they had open gaping wounds; today many wounds are not so spectacular as they are lethal. Then, wounds tended to be on the upper part of the body; today many are in the legs and lower abdomen. Then, it was a disgrace - or took some explaining away - to be wounded from behind; today it is a frequent occurrence.

THE BATTLE OF NORTHAMPTON
10 July 1460

Within a year Henry had reasserted himself as a Monarch and dismissed the Yorkists from the posts they had assumed. York himself did not greatly care, for his arch-enemy Somerset was dead, and he had no personal ambition for the throne. But there were other forces at work. There were the powerful barons who needed to act to demonstrate their own importance to themselves and their followers, and there was Queen Margaret, who hated York and saw him as a threat to the chance of her own son succeeding to the throne. For three years she spent most of her time travelling and campaigning for support in the next, inevitable, clash.

Bloodshed began again when Margaret tried to have Warwick, the architect of victory at St Albans, assassinated in a provoked incident when he was visiting London. During the years after that battle she had won over a number of supporters, in Hereford, Gloucester and Cheshire. She had conferred on them the badge of Prince Edward, which was a silver swan, and it is said that many were so beguiled that they would have accepted the young prince as their monarch in place of his father. As York himself lived at Ludlow, Shropshire, and she had concentrated her energies on to the adjoining counties, notably Chester, this was carrying the war into the enemy's country and giving a challenge that would not be ignored. Warwick's father, the Earl of Salisbury, set off with 3,000 men to join the Duke of York at Ludlow. Henry and Margaret heard of it, and called on their supporters to counter the threat. The king's representative was Lord Audley and he intercepted the Yorkists on 3 September at Blore Heath, two and a half miles east of Market Drayton. It was a grim and bloody battle, in which Lord Audley was killed, and - it was said - caused the stream to run red with blood for three days. The Yorkists were outnumbered but must have handled their forces with greater skill than the Lancastrians.

This was all that was needed. England was once more plunged into civil war. The Yorkists centred on Ludlow while the Lancastrians assembled their army at Worcester. This was apparently the first and last time that Henry looked and behaved like the son of his famous warrior father. Nevertheless he did not lose his diplomatic or compassionate quality and gave his opponents every chance to avoid the next battle by offering free pardons to all his would-be opponents. The Yorkists, well aware of Queen Margaret's probable clemency to those in her power, shifted their feet uneasily, and said they had no quarrel with his royal personage but they would like other assurances before they disbanded their army. Henry was not pleased and set his own forces marching forward. Intelligent though he was he could not appreciate that his particular circle of advisers was so hostile to the Yorkists that unless he dismissed half of them and replaced them with nominees from the other side, peace was impossible.

Surprisingly enough the ultimate defeat of the king was obscured and delayed at this point. There was still uncertainty in the Yorkist ranks and when the news circulated that they could go home with a free pardon, rather than try conclusion with a force which was said to outnumber them by ten to one, many of them slipped away during the night. This was the Battle of Ludford, the battle which was not a battle. The Yorkist army dispersed. York fled to Ireland; Warwick, Salisbury, the Earl of March (York's eldest son) and Sir John Wenlock, who will figure spectacularly, but not fortunately, in a later battle, rode desperately to Devonshire. From Devon they had a most difficult journey to safety at Calais, and would not have reached it at all had Warwick not taken the tiller personally.

The Yorkist rout looked worse than it was. Warwick controlled Calais and a useful fleet; York was supreme in Ireland. In terms of real power they were far superior to the king for they controlled the trade routes in and out of the kingdom. Meanwhile Henry's army made itself vastly unpopular by sacking Ludlow, and followed this by the sacking of Newbury for no better reason than that it was supposed to favour the Yorkists. Henry held a form of

Parliament at Coventry which merely seemed a legislative device for oppressing those of his opponents who had a legitimate grievance.

The news of what was afoot was not lost on Warwick and the other Yorkist exiles. At the first moment which seemed opportune Warwick landed at Calais and moved swiftly inland, but not so swiftly that he did not recruit numerous supporters in Kent. Support in London was excellent and Warwick marched in to the capital unopposed. The swift and successful Yorkist return was a shock for the Lancastrians but they were not too disconcerted, nor too unprepared. They still had loyal supporters even in predominantly Yorkist areas. In London Lord Hungerford and Lord Scales retired with their forces to the Tower of London and blazed away in all directions with their cannon. However, possession of the Tower was not vital to Yorkist success and Warwick's army did not pause long. Victory and a change of government could come by pitched battle only, so he lost no time in setting out to confront the royal army, and its adherents.

The Lancastrians were strong in the Midlands, and had supporters they could rely on in the north and west. Nevertheless, when Warwick set out marching north-west from London on 5 July rumours were flying ahead that his force was unbeatable. The foundation for this overstatement seems to be that they had obtained the support of the Papal Legate and also the Archbishop of Canterbury, as well as a number of other religious leaders. It is said that Henry, who was now going through one of his periodic lapses, was too feeble in mind to grasp the extent of the physical and spiritual power arrayed against him but many of his supporters did and a number found their consciences so disturbed that they slipped away to become neutrals, holding themselves in readiness to join the winning side.

Northampton is sixty-six miles from London so without much pressure the Yorkists were able to reach it by the ninth. Thirty-two miles north-west of Northampton lay Coventry, which the Lancastrians had used as their Midlands seat of government. The Lancastrian army had moved south-east out of Coventry to confront the Yorkists but had prudently sent Queen Margaret and her young son back to Eccleshall in Staffordshire, thereby placing them about seventy miles behind the danger zone and in a district where they had numerous friends.

The Lancastrian strategy was partly intentional, and partly forced upon them. It was their ambition to confront the Yorkists and defeat them, but as there was by now a disparity in numbers (the Yorkist army being given as 7,000, and the Lancastrian as 5,000) as well as a considerable advantage in morale on the Yorkist side, the Lancastrians decided to take up an entrenched position. If the Yorkists now attacked they would be at the disadvantage of attacking a prepared defence, which normally requires a three to one superiority (if success is going to be likely). If they did not attack the royal army they would leave it between them and the capital, and would be caught between it and other Lancastrian forces which would now be marching from the north and west. The royal army therefore took up a position inside a bend of the river Nene, which was a broad river in those days. (The Nene, up till recently, was known as the 'Nen'.) The exact position is not accurately known for it is said that the river has changed its course a little since those days, but is sometimes identified as the site of the Avon factory.

However, when we reflect that 5,000 men were in the entrenched position it is obvious that the royalist army could have occupied not merely one but several bends. In medieval warfare a man needed at least a yard and a half of frontage, perhaps even two yards, if he was not to do more damage to his own side than the enemy while swinging his weapons. The reader may prove this to himself by simply swinging a tennis racket and seeing how much ground he requires if he is not to injure the nearest person. So if the royal army was five deep it could still have required a frontage of a mile. In fact, it was probably ten deep and extended over half a mile.

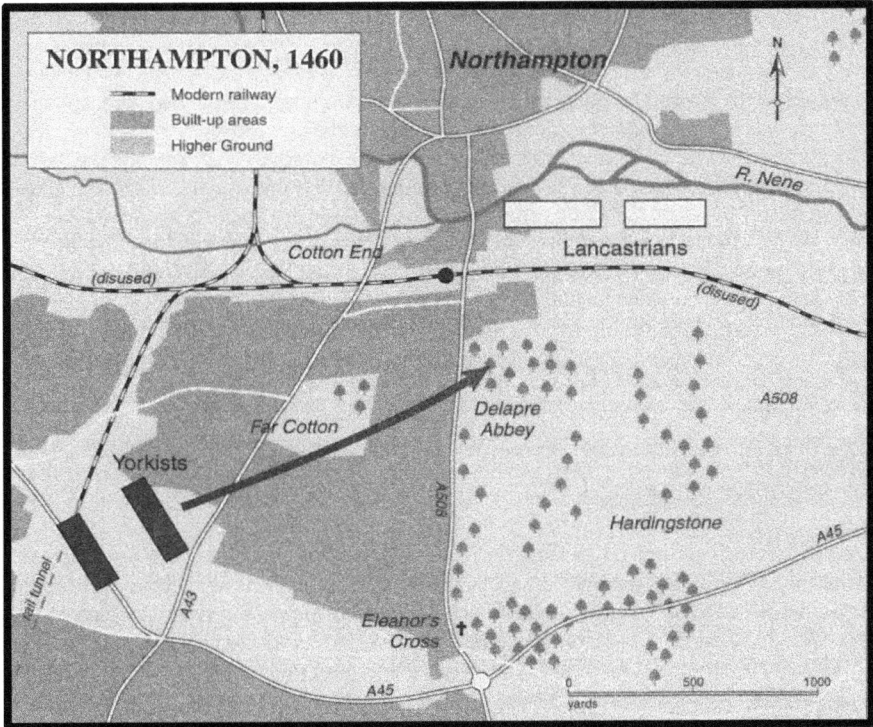

NORTHAMPTON, 1460

Modern railway
Built-up areas
Higher Ground

Northampton

N

R. Nene

(disused)

Cotton End

Lancastrians

(disused)

A508

Delapre
Abbey

Far Cotton

Yorkists

Hardingstone

A45

rail tunnel

A43

A508

Eleanor's
Cross

A45

0   500   1000
yards

It is advisable to go along the A508 road and inspect the meadows on the Delapre Abbey side (Northamptonshire).

The exact date of the Lancastrian army's arrival in Northampton is not precisely known but it seems that it was in sufficient time to make a considerable defensive position, with banks and trenches. We may have some doubts about the depth of the trenches for the area is wet and marshy today, and was undoubtedly much worse then. The fact that the ensuing battle was fought in pouring rain cannot have added to the value of the trenches as fire points although it certainly helped to impede the advancing Yorkist infantry The choice of position had considerable advantages but substantial liabilities. It was a tactical position the French had frequently used in the late wars and the English had reason to respect it but such a site requires some luck if it is going to be successful. And Henry was not a man to create luck.

An interesting feature of this battle - and many other battles of the Wars of the Roses - was that non-combatants rarely became involved. Law and order had to a large extent broken down but both sides had the sense not to involve merchants and trades-people in their quarrels. The Lancastrians could - had they wished - have occupied and defended the town, which had a very strong castle, but this would have involved hardship and bloodshed among the innocent; and as it was not the policy of either army to alienate civilians, on whom they relied for supplies, the battle was fought outside the town. It could easily have taken place on Hunsbury Hill, an old Danish camp, but the Lancastrians preferred the river site, and Hunsbury was left for Warwick to occupy as his headquarters on the night of the ninth. The following morning he made a tentative attempt at a negotiated peace by sending the Bishop of Salisbury to see Henry but it was obvious to both sides that this was an issue which could only be settled by battle. Salisbury returned without speaking to the king. Warwick therefore led out his army along the old drove road towards Hardingstone Meadow (or Newfield -or Cow Meadow). They skirted the grounds of the Delapre Abbey and came down towards the entrenchments by the river. On their way they passed the Queen Eleanor Cross, which Edward I had put there when his wife's coffin had rested at that spot on the way to burial in Westminster Abbey in 1290. (Charing Cross was the last of the long line of Eleanor Crosses). It is said that the Archbishop of Canterbury and the Papal Legate stood together on the mound bearing the cross and watched the battle. Today the cross is surrounded by trees, and it is impossible to test this interesting claim, but it seems unlikely that they could have had much of a view over several fields in pouring rain. What they may have seen was some of the outlying skirmishes.

It seems that owing to the rain, the marsh, and the perimeter defences which were by now ditches filled with water, the main attack did not begin till 2p.m. The assault may not have been intended at all for it must have seemed to the Yorkists impossible to break through the watery defences which during the Middle Ages had over and over again proved themselves better than any stone and mortar. But inevitably there were the probing frontline troops who were inspired by the thoughts of reward as well as threats from their captains immediately behind. The Lancastrian archers had a fine time with the Yorkist mounted troops, whose horses stuck in the mud; those armoured men who reached the rampart found it impossible to climb the slippery sides. Honours were still even, for the handguns - and larger guns too - which the Lancastrians had relied on to terrify any Yorkists who came to close quarters had become wet in the rain and would not fire. For half an hour the battle hung in the balance, then, as often happened in these wars, treachery led to the decision. The right of the Lancastrian position was commanded by Lord Grey. His efforts had not been very striking but had at least been adequate; on the left Buckingham was going much better and it looked as if he might soon make a sally and begin to slaughter the floundering Yorkists. Suddenly - although it must have been by prearranged signal - Grey's men were seen to be assisting the Yorkists into their lines. Baron Fauconberg, who commanded the Yorkist left wing, then ensured that Warwick, commanding the Yorkist centre, and the Earl of March (later to be Edward IV) would soon follow.

It is said that Warwick gave orders that the nobility only were to be killed, and the rank and file should be spared. This was not a time in which men gave much heed to promises, and the Lancastrian soldiers mostly decided to take their chance of crossing the river. This, of course, was in flood, and as many of them were forced to chance the passage by the mill where the current was swiftest, many were drowned. Nevertheless the casualties seem surprisingly light in relation to the numbers involved. The figure of 300 is given but this can hardly include those drowned trying to cross the river. But the roll call looks impressive enough for it included Buckingham, Shrewsbury, Beaumont, and Egremont. Henry, again, narrowly escaped injury, and was taken into custody by a Yorkist archer. He was subsequently treated with courtesy, but kept under surveillance in London. When he arrived the Tower was still holding out but surrendered two days later (18 July).

Lord Scales was released, and promised a safe passage but was murdered while in a boat on the river; the war had by now become bitter and treacherous, and no one trusted promises whether by his own side or the enemy's. Scales' body had apparently lain on the ground in a Southwark cemetery 'naked as a worm'. Warwick had not ordered the murder but is blamed for not having issued firm orders to prevent it. One of Scales' custodians had been Sir John Wenlock, and this incident may well have been remembered on the battlefield at Tewkesbury (see The Battle of Tewkesbury).

Northampton seems to have been an occasion when men settled a few private scores. A contemporary writer described how Sir William Lucy, who lived near the battlefield, came to see what assistance he could give to the royal party as they seemed to be in trouble. He was promptly killed by John Stafford, a Yorkist who was in love with Lucy's wife, whom subsequently he married.

On hearing news of the disaster Queen Margaret fled for safety to North Wales. She had a difficult journey. Near Malpas castle in Cheshire she was intercepted by a Yorkist but escaped. Later her own servants turned against her and robbed her of her money and jewels but she was rescued by a fourteen-year-old boy John Combe of Amesbury who took her to safety at Harlech. Subsequently she moved to Denbigh Castle where she had the protection of the Earl of Pembroke, and was able to begin rebuilding her forces. Many of her most powerful supporters had not been at Northampton and she was still able to call on such formidable allies as the dukes of Somerset and Exeter, the Earls of Wiltshire and Northumberland, and 'the butcher', Lord Clifford.

Attempts were made to lure the Queen out of her fastness in order to visit King Henry but she was not deceived. Towards the end of 1460 she went by ship to Scotland where she betrothed her son to the daughter of the Scottish Queen (1), and handed over the town of Berwick in return for Scottish support in her forthcoming struggles. Meanwhile the Duke of York, who had been in Ireland since the fiasco at Ludford, now returned and laid claim to the throne. His bid was not a success. Although Henry was known to be mad, and his supporters had made themselves thoroughly unpopular, he was still considered the rightful king. The Duke of York had a slightly stronger claim in that he was the nearest living relative to the murdered Richard n, but that event had happened over sixty years ago and nobody had disputed the Lancastrian title since. Furthermore the Lancastrian title to the throne had been confirmed by Act of Parliament, and any fresh contender had to obtain its consent before he had any status in the eyes of the country as a whole. As a state of war still existed, and the crowned king was still alive, even if mad, it was unlikely that there could be much enthusiasm for the Duke of York. He recognized the fact himself and although Parliament accepted that he was now the de facto king he had the sense to style himself Protector.

(1) The king, James n of Scotland, had been killed when one of his cannons burst while he was besieging Roxburgh Castle on 3 August.

However by this time York had made the fatal mistakes which led to his ruin. Instead of driving north after the victory of Northampton he had wasted valuable time. When he moved in December it was too late; the Lancastrians were now reorganized and in great strength. On 30 December just outside Sandal Castle, Wakefield,

York's army was massacred, and he himself was killed. Two thousand five hundred Yorkists were killed for the loss of 200 Lancastrians. Queen Margaret had the heads of the leading Yorkists set above the gateway to York with the Duke's head in the middle wearing a paper crown.   The war had now become revengeful and bitter, far removed from the courtesy of the first Battle of St Albans. And there was worse to come.

THE BATTLE OF MORTIMER'S CROSS
2 February 1461

Wakefield though a disaster to the Yorkists, was not the end of their hopes. Although York would be difficult to replace, for he was moderate and statesmanlike, there were other good men on the Yorkist side, and plenty of supporters who believed England had a better future with the Yorkists than with mad King Henry and his embittered wife. Now that York was dead the next heir to the throne on the Yorkist side was the Earl of March, who had commanded the right wing at Northampton, and his brother Richard of Gloucester. The Earl of March would become Edward IV and Richard would become Richard m, the alleged murderer of the princes in the Tower.

The Earl of March, who will from now on be referred to as Edward, was at Shrewsbury when the Battle of Wakefield was being fought; he was waiting there to forestall any attempt the Earl of Pembroke might make to make a swift drive into England. On hearing the news of Wakefield and realizing that the Lancastrians would waste no time in following up their victory with a march to London, he increased his army to set off to intercept them. If he linked up with Warwick's forces he would probably be able to cripple the Lancastrians, and slow them down, if not actually to defeat them. But when he reached Hereford he was overtaken by other more serious news. The Earl of Pembroke had now begun to march, in company with the Earl of Wiltshire and a strong supporting army of Irish, Bretons, French, and Welsh. Edward turned back. If Pembroke's army reached the Midlands the Yorkist cause might be as good as won. Edward was not the man to flinch from the right decision, however upsetting it might be to his former plans.

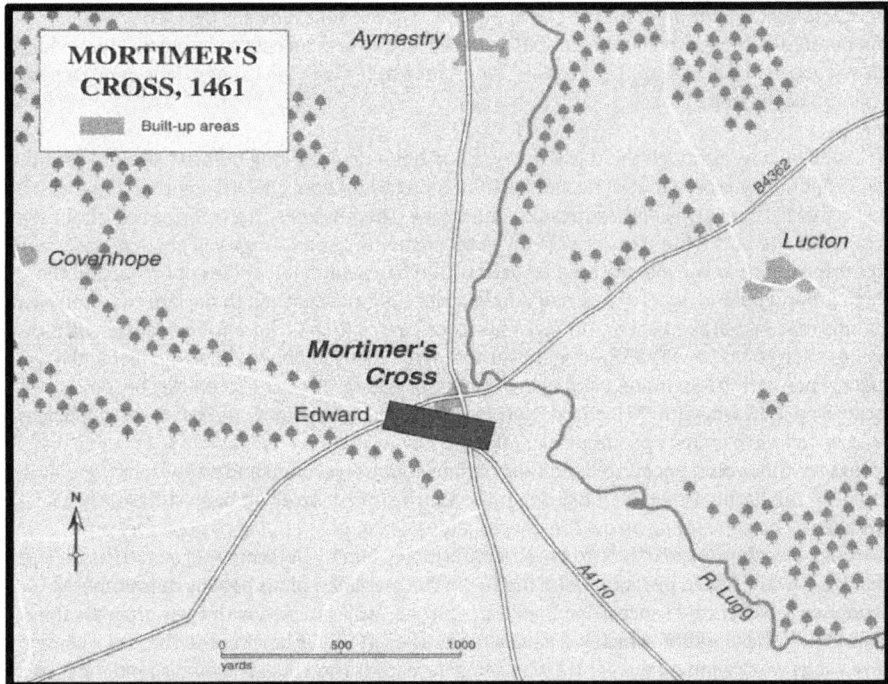

MORTIMER'S
CROSS, 1461

Built-up areas

Aymestry

Lucton

Covenhope

Mortimer's
Cross

Edward

N

0 500 1000
yards

The battlefield is very easy to find. Go to the junction of the A4110 and the B4362 roads (Herefordshire)

The ensuing battle took place at Mortimer's Cross, Herefordshire. Edward's force was not one to inspire great confidence for it had nothing comparable in battle experience to the opposition. He made his dispositions in Wig Marsh, close to what is now known as Mortimer's Cross. In the inn at the crossroads there is a map of the battlefield, and this is by no means the only asset to recommend it. It is said that Sir Richard Croft, who lived in Croft Castle nearby, advised Edward how to make his dispositions, and advised the future king to let the Lancastrians attack. As Edward's army was now skillfully disposed in what was then marshy ground, but which is now meadow, this was reasonable enough. Nevertheless Edward's position seems to have some liabilities and he appears lucky to have got away with it. All his forces were to the west of the river Lugg which was some twenty feet across at that time of the year. Edward himself commanded the centre battle which held the bridge. The explanation of the tactical dispositions - and the reader may have a better one - seems to be that Edward wished to block the Lancastrian advance and was prepared to expend some of his troops in doing so. As he had greater numbers, though they were less well-equipped than his opponents, he could afford to be lavish in expending them.

The battle was preceded by a remarkable omen, or so it must have seemed. By some meteorological phenomenon the sun appeared as three suns. Edward decided it was a favourable auspice, which represented both the Trinity and success to his own side. He knelt down and said a prayer of thanksgiving. As he rose to his feet the Lancastrians approached and the battle began.

It lasted all day, although the decisive point had been reached long before darkness, and the later fighting was only that of desperate men trying to escape. Edward commanded the centre of his own army and confronted Pembroke. There is very little information about the course of the battle but it is not difficult to reconstruct. It seems highly likely that apart from his dispositions in the marshy area Edward would have stationed bodies of archers on the high ground behind, where they had ample cover until they wished to declare themselves. It seems that Pembroke kept a portion of his force confronting Edward in the centre while the wings tried to find a way around and over the river. Such a manoeuvre would be highly dangerous with badly trained and ill-disciplined troops for they would quickly become scattered. Edward, with Sir Richard Croft to guide him, would know the best crossing places and would have archers positioned to rake them with fire. He could afford to sacrifice his wings for this would encourage the Lancastrians to press forward and sway from the critical point of the battle. When he judged that the Lancastrian centre had been sufficiently weakened by converging arrow fire, by casualties sustained in trying to push forward through treacherous marsh onto prepared positions, and by detachments sent to assist the flanks, Edward would press forward and begin the massacre of his heavily outnumbered opponents. When the Lancastrian flankers returned, well satisfied with their progress they would find the situation which we have already seen at Lewes and in other battles - while the wings were winning the centre was being defeated. The Yorkists would spend most of their time trapping and killing small parties of Lancastrians. Many of those who managed to escape from the immediate area of the battlefield would have short shrift, for this was a Yorkist area, and small wonder that the number of Lancastrian dead was given as 3,000; this may have been over half their army. Doubtless they had set out in smaller numbers than was safe, confident that all that was required of them was to join up with the victors of Wakefield, and take part in the general plundering and massacre. They could hardly have imagined that Edward, with his father so recently killed, and the Yorkists in disarray, would be able to recruit a large and enthusiastic army. They were also, had they but known it, confronting one of the great military tacticians of the century. Not least of the reasons for their defeat would be surprise at finding their way blocked by so large a force.

After the battle no mercy was shown to the defeated leaders. The most spectacular killing was that of Owen Tudor, father of the Earl of Pembroke. After Henry V had died, Tudor, who was then a Welsh country squire, had married his widow. His son had been created Earl of Pembroke and his most famous descendant would be Henry Tudor, who would become Henry VII. But all that was of little avail after the battle of Mortimer's Cross. He was taken to Haverford west market place and beheaded.

Haverfordwest is the place given in a contemporary account, and as it is in Pembrokeshire it would appear to be eminently suitable for the public execution of the father of the earl, but other accounts give the scene as Hereford, which would certainly be more convenient, through being nearer. Haverfordwest or Hereford, it made no difference to Owen Tudor. He did not believe he could be beheaded until he saw the axe and the block, and even then he had doubts, thinking that perhaps it was all a device to frighten him, and there would be a last minute reprieve. But when his executioner ripped off the collar of his red velvet doublet, so that it should not deflect the axe, he realized it was all over. Philosophically, he said 'That head shall lie on the stock that was wont to lie on Queen Catherine's lap.' After his death his head was put on the market cross, but it was taken down by a woman, said to be mad, who washed the blood off the face, combed the hair and surrounded it with more than a hundred lighted candles.

Today the battlefield of Mortimer's Cross is easily recognisable, although there are now hedges which did not exist when it was fought. The best starting point is at the intersection of the A4110 and the B4362. If the reader comes down the road from Presteigne he will realise how great was the shock to the Lancastrians. Either they had to press on and cross the river, or turn right and move along the old Watling Street and Leominster road. Either way they were at a disadvantage. They had one other course but no one seems to have thought of it. Perhaps the reader will see this, and others Edward, although only eighteen years old, was experienced enough in battle to know that one victory was not enough and there were other urgent tasks on hand. Nevertheless, on this occasion he seems to have displayed a little of that lethargy which sometimes affected him. In a crisis he could drive himself and others like a superhuman but once the immediate danger was passed would waste time in dissipation. By the time he displayed his next burst of energy another disaster had overtaken the Yorkists. This was the Second Battle of St Albans.

THE SECOND BATTLE OF ST ALBANS
12 February 1461

After Wakefield Queen Margaret had rewarded and reorganized her forces: she had not hurried matters, possible because the near disastrous defeat of Northampton was still present in her mind. The victory at Wakefield had been due to careful preparation and planning; the question now was what was the best course of action.

The king, although useless as a warrior, was still in Yorkist hands, and could perhaps be used by them in bargaining. It was therefore expedient to rescue him as quickly as possible. Once the decision was taken there was no delay. With a large army, which was said to contain Scots, Welsh, and French, she set off south.

This march of the Lancastrians was one of the few occasions when the war really affected the civilian population. Possibly her motley force was out of control, possibly she was letting them do as they wished on the principle of terrorizing the countryside and softening up the opposition with fear and rumour. When the English armies had fought in France during the Hundred Years' War the policy of 'havoc'- that is, to devastate the countryside and spread terror, had been frequently followed. Each town the Lancastrian army passed through had good reason to remember the experience: Grantham, Stamford, Peterborough, Huntingdon and Royston were especially mentioned. At Dunstable they clashed with a party of Yorkists, said to have been commanded by the town butcher. The Lancastrian army was too much for it; the Yorkists had 200 killed and the butcher hanged himself for shame.

Meanwhile Warwick was arranging for their reception, and doubtless hoping that Edward would come up to assist him. In the event, matters turned out slightly differently.

The battle which is known as the Second Battle of St Albans is of great interest and complexity. The first battle, described earlier, was straightforward, though interesting enough. The second is full of puzzles.

The Lancastrian army was advancing down the route of the AI but for some unknown reason Queen Margaret turned west and came on to what is now the A5. In all probability she realized that her coming and her likely route into London would be anticipated. This swerve would have an element of surprise.

Warwick, however, was not deceived. Doubtless his scouts were keeping him well-informed. When he knew the Lancastrians were swerving left he realised they were sure to come though St Albans. A victory there would wipe out the former defeat of the Lancastrians when Henry had been wounded and taken prisoner. Warwick was fairly confident of victory and took the king with him to St Albans. The widow of the late Duke of York was less confident and she sent her two younger sons to Holland. These were George, Duke of Clarence, later to be drowned in a butt of Malmsey wine, and Richard of Gloucester, who later became Richard III.

It has been said that Margaret's tactical manoeuvres on the road to St Albans were unique for the period but this is not by any means true. There were, however, two features which made her manoeuvres more effective. One was that she swerved across the front of the enemy position, and then doubled back; the other was that to double back she made a night march, and followed it with a dawn attack. Night marches are an attractive idea, as are night attacks; the problem with a night march is that men can go astray, desert, or injure themselves on rough ground; and the hazard of a night attack is that an army may well attack some portion of its own side by mistake in the darkness.

However, events went well for Margaret. Her army completed the twelve miles from Dunstable to St Albans without mishap and it is said that they reached their destination well before dawn. As they came to the town they crossed the site of the old Roman city of Verulamium and came up George Street. It is probable that they fanned out and came in on each side of the abbey but after the first surprise they were confronted with deadly arrow fire and could get no further. For the second time in this war the narrowness of the streets was proving a decisive factor, for the Lancastrian advance was funneled into a perfect killing ground for the Yorkist archers. Checked and dismayed the Lancastrians fell back. Their beautiful flanking move had achieved initial surprise but now seemed to have been checked.

As the Lancastrians very well knew, the main Yorkist army was not in the town at all but spread thinly as a screen to the north. Warwick's front line was nearly four miles long, but he had strong detachments on the main roads. Not surprisingly he took advantage of the old Belgae ditch defences that had been constructed in pre-Roman times. Along this he had laid various devices of the type that were well enough known in close defences but had rarely been used in open warfare. Among them were caltraps, which were four spikes jointed together so that however they fell on the ground one would be pointing upwards. They were cheap and easy to make and could be sown in thousands. They were deadly to men but especially disconcerting to cavalry. They also laid cord netting with spikes at each corner which could be concealed under leaves in pathways, or gaps through hedges.

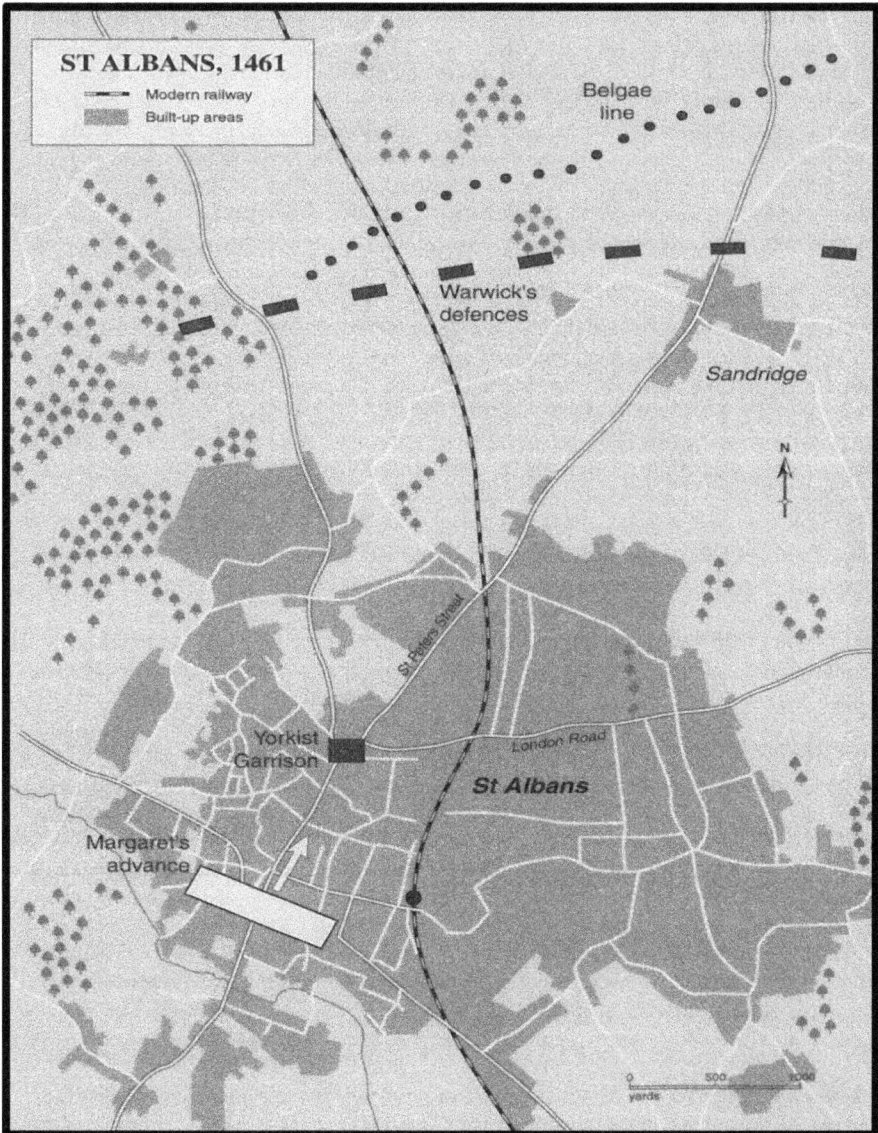

ST ALBANS, 1461

━ ━ Modern railway
Built-up areas

Belgae line

Warwick's defences

Sandridge

N

St Peters Street

Yorkist Garrison

London Road

St Albans

Margaret's advance

0   500   1000
yards

It is best to begin the battlefield tour in the town and then move out on Harpenden road. Sandridge, Beech Bottom and Wheathampstead are easily found, and it is possible to follow the course of the old Belgae line. (Hertfordshire).

Another feature was the use made of pavises. A pavis was a wooden or hide shield carried on a crossbowman's back. He would shelter behind it while winding up his crossbow, and also, sometimes, use it for a guard when shooting. On this occasion the pavises were studded with sharp protruding nails so that when the archer had fired off all his bolts (or quarrels as they were often called), he could lay down his pavis and make walking very hazardous for his opponents. (There are some pavises in the Fitzwilliam Museum in Cambridge.) The Yorkists also had handguns. These were carried by Burgundian mercenaries, and were meant to shoot darts and arrows. However they were more of a morale-raiser than an effective weapon. Rain would put them out of action, a stiff breeze would blow away the powder, they might discharge unpredictably if badly packed; and loading took the best part of half an hour. Two shots an hour against a longbow which can manage twelve shots a minute is not effective for long. Eighteen were said to have been burned to death by flames from their own guns. The Yorkists also had some cannon but these again were less effective than intimidating. For the moment, however, the main Lancastrian force was not engaged.

By now the tactical dispositions had become a commander's nightmare. The Yorkist detachment in the centre of the town - in St Peter's Street - had Lancastrians on both sides of it, some from George Street, some from Folly Lane. Equally the northern group of Lancastrians had Yorkists on each side, and as Warwick sent some of the outlying defenders back to the town the situation looked unhealthy for the Lancastrians.

At this point the Lancastrians nearly lost the battle. Their proper course was to leave a small detachment engaging the Yorkist garrison, thus preventing it linking up with the vanguard under Warwick. But - possibly because their minds were dull after a night march and a dawn attack - they played for apparent safety, and concentrated on eliminating the town garrison. This provided a situation in complete contrast to the First Battle of St Albans. Then the Yorkists were trying to capture the Lancastrian-held centre with an attack from the south; now the Lancastrians were trying to defeat a Yorkist-held town with an attack from the north. Another contrast between the two battles was that in the earlier one the twenty-five-year-old Earl of Warwick had shown great fire and initiative, possibly because he was keen to attack and make his name; now at thirty-two he seemed to have lost his impetus in the complexity of making an elaborate defensive plan. It may of course be borne in mind - but not by misogynists - that Queen Margaret was a first-class general, better than Warwick and all the other Yorkists except Edward. Undoubtedly she was the architect of the surprising Lancastrian victory at Wakefield, and the fact that her armies were beaten at Towton and Tewkesbury seems more a matter of bad luck than bad judgement.

As may be expected the Yorkist garrison did not submit to elimination very easily or quickly. As the holders of the town they had cleared fields of fire from the windows of the houses overlooking the street, and their archers were able to do a vast amount of damage before they were killed. Medieval St Albans offered excellent facilities for the stubborn defenders of doorways, passages and staircases. Even today, with the aid of grenades and other forms of explosives, clearing a street of snipers and others is by no means a simple and quick procedure. By the time the last Yorkist had been slaughtered it was midday. Warwick, as the Yorkist commander, was in an awkward position. He could of course have sent a detachment to harass the Lancastrians before they killed off the Yorkist garrison in the town. But if he did so he would be weakening his already dispersed and scattered force. There was no doubt that by coming up on the flank, and surprising him both in timing and position, Margaret had sent his plans staggering. He therefore had to regroup before his detachments were overrun. His careful defences were now likely to be a bigger hazard to his own side than to the enemy. His whole army, once collected, had to be turned round to face in the opposite direction. Hastily they moved the nets, and pavises, though there was nothing they could do about the caltraps.

When the armies met again the fighting was stubborn and blood y, though showing signs of weariness. Some of the vaunted Yorkist handguns blew up in their users' hands, and some incendiary arrows came back to their own side, but they were intimidating to the Lancastrians for all that. It began to snow. The scene on the battlefield was now indescribably confused, but more and more Lancastrians were coming up with a taste of success on their lips, and more and more Yorkists were getting lost in the general disarray. To add to Yorkist discomfiture Captain Lovelace changed sides at the critical moment and took his Kentish men over to the Lancastrian side. This and other actions - such as that of Grey at Northampton - made this a war in which a man could hardly trust his neighbour. Finally the Yorkist left wing gave way and fled. It was a chilling sight for the remainder but Warwick then showed something of his true quality. He rallied his own centre column, collected what was still left of the right wing, and held a ridge until dark. Once night fell it was almost impossible to tell friend from foe; he managed to extricate 4,000 of his followers and march them to Chipping Norton, Oxfordshire. The king was not with him. Once again Henry VI was sitting by himself, smiling patiently and uncomprehendingly. He was taken to St Albans Abbey.

The numbers engaged in this battle are given as 10,000 on each side. It sounds a suspiciously round figure but may not be far from the truth. When medieval chroniclers wished to indicate huge but unknown numbers they would describe them as 60,000 men, and this had much the same significance as the modern '64,000 dollar question'. The Yorkist casualties were undoubtedly heavy, and it seems unlikely that Warwick could have got away with 4,000 unwounded men; for that number the Yorkist army would probably have needed to have been over 10,000 strong at the outset. The probable figure is that there were 2,000 Yorkists left on the field and about another 2,000 accompanied Warwick. Some perhaps went home and decided they had had enough of battles and fighting.

The young Prince of Wales, aged seven, was knighted on the field.

By all accounts he was an unpleasant child, doubtless made so by his embittered mother. He was given the task of deciding how captured Yorkists should die, and happily assigned this one to the axe, this one to the hangman, and that to the sword. Not surprisingly when his own turn came ten years later he received no mercy either.

A more commendable record was that of Andrew Trollope, who was also knighted. He had stepped on a caltrap early in the fight and been somewhat inconvenienced. As he put it, 'he had only managed to kill fifteen men'. Trollope was an old soldier who had originally been a Yorkist but who had joined the Lancastrians after Ludford.

The visitor to St Albans will need plenty of time if he is to walk both battles. The second is clearly the more complicated and he will need to move well out to Barnard's Heath (sometimes called Barnet Heath) to Beech Bottom, and to Sandridge. The centre of the town has, like many others, changed in appearance in recent years but it is still possible to obtain a clear idea of the battles as they were fought 500 years ago.

THE BATTLE OF BARNET
14 April 1471

The Lancastrian victory at St Albans could have ended the war if it had been followed up. It is said that Henry VI prevailed on Margaret not to let loose the wild northerners on the capital. The Lancastrian army included in its ranks fighting men from the depths of the Highlands, and Borderers who spent their lives in fighting, and it was felt, and not only by Henry, that once they were inside the city walls there would be no end to their plundering and destruction; it was feared that the city itself might be burnt to the ground. Also the city was already hostile and might put up a fierce resistance, enabling Edward to come up with his army.

But the decision was fatal to the Lancastrian cause. While Queen Margaret's army waited at St Albans, and the city was sending delegates to negotiate its surrender, Edward arrived on the scene. Having delayed a little after Mortimer's Cross he had now made up for it. A forced march brought him to London and completely transformed the military situation. Instead of facing an apparently defenceless city the Lancastrians were confronting a victorious army, which had already been supplemented by the forces Warwick had extricated from the recent battle.

Once the opportunity had been lost there was no point in staying at St Albans. There was no food for an army, and the northerners were already making their own arrangements by plundering far and wide. Had Edward driven forward immediately he could have reversed the previous decision; Margaret who was only too alert to swift vicissitudes from triumph to disaster was not to be caught. Gathering up her forces, who seemed to regard the entire country south of the Trent as enemy territory, she fell back towards York. This move led to the greatest battle of the Wars of the Roses. Edward pushed up north after her as fast as he could, and eventually overhauled her army at Towton near Tadcaster. That great and bloody battle is described in the second book in this series. At the end of it 35,000 dead were said to be left on the field. The real figure may be one-third of that number but there can be no doubt that the slaughter was enormous. For once, almost everyone concerned was on the field, and the winner took all. Subsequently there were, of course, pockets of resistance which had to be crushed, and there were two sizeable battles in 1464 but the Lancastrians seemed crushed for the time being. Although Henry VI was still alive - he was not murdered till 1471 - Edward IV became king and his title was recognized by Parliament. It seemed that all was set fair for the Yorkists.

But, as often happens, the great military commander was not really interested in the problems of peace. When not fighting he merely interested himself in clothes, women and drink. His capacity for women and drinking was phenomenal, although it seems to have led to an early death at the age of forty-one. A night's carousing with Edward - now Edward IV - was a prospect which would make the hardest drinker blench. What his numerous mistresses thought of his amatory prowess is not recorded, but at least ten of his children were legitimate.

Fortunately, again as often happens, there was someone at hand who enjoyed the work which Edward detested. This was Warwick, now known as 'the King Maker'. He was immensely rich and fond of power; in fact he was richer than the king himself. One of the factors which contributed to the long continuance of the Wars of the Roses was the enormous wealth possessed by certain families. The reasons lay far back in time and do not concern us but the effects, of course, do.

Warwick, of course, had good reason to think highly of himself. He had been consistently loyal and more often than not had helped to turn the scales in Yorkist favour. But when he attempted to crown his efforts by marrying Edward to a suitable bride he was surprised and disgusted to hear that the king was married already; in secret, so as not to arouse the animosity of his family, he had married the widow of a Lancastrian. When Warwick showed indignation Ed- ward laughed at him. His bride's family (the Woodvilles) were flaunted and loaded with titles and honours. It was meant to show Warwick that he was not indispensable but it had a greater effect than intended.

Warwick's reaction was to plot with the Duke of Clarence, Edward's brother. Clarence was a dubious character who seemed to like nobody, but he was jealous of his brother and was happy to plot with Warwick. Eventually their efforts brought open war and at the Battle of Edgcote Field, near Banbury (1469) Edward was beaten and taken prisoner. Later he was released on the assurance that he would rule according to the wishes of Clarence and Warwick.

It was an unlikely possibility. Edward was given permission to raise an army to deal with Lancastrian rebellion but then turned it against Warwick and Clarence. Caught unprepared they were lucky to get out of the country.

'Hell hath no fury like a woman scorned' unless perhaps it be a disgruntled King Maker. Warwick promptly set off to treat with Queen Margaret, and restore Henry to the throne. Henry was by now a poor wretched thing, but no matter. Margaret hated and distrusted Warwick but after much hesitation she agreed to her son being betrothed to Warwick's daughter. Once more Edward was caught unawares, although again he would be quick to recover. When Warwick and Clarence landed in 1470 the tide of Lancastrian support rose so quickly that Edward had to escape to Flanders. Henry VI, said to be as animated as a sack of potatoes, was taken from his dungeon and made king. The Lancastrians had triumphed again. But Edward had not been beaten, only discomfited. Having raised money and men on the Continent he landed at Spurhead in Yorkshire in 1471. He moved swiftly to London in one of his now famous marches. Clarence, who should have intercepted him from the west, decided instead to betray his father-in-law, and joined his brother. Edward marched into London and Henry VI was once more his prisoner.

Warwick's conduct during Edward's march south had been vacillating and surprising. Twice he could have confronted him and given battle, once with superior numbers. Possibly he felt that if Edward marched around enough he would lose more supporters than he gained; or perhaps he hoped to cut him off in the south. Unfortunately for the Lancastrian s, when Warwick took action it was too little and too late.

On 12 April Edward, who was now in London, heard that Warwick was approaching with a huge force. Edward wasted no time. On the thirteenth he was setting out north to meet Warwick, and the unfortunate Henry was taken along with him.

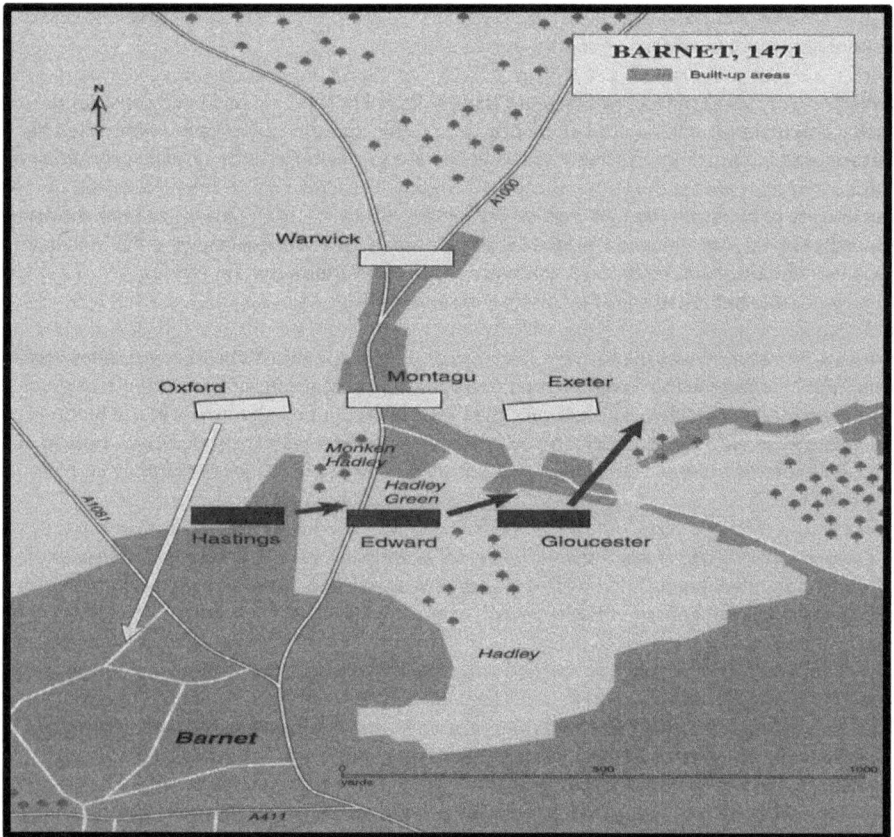

BARNET, 1471
Built-up areas

Travel up the A1000 from Barnet to Hadley Green. Turn right at Hadley Green for the line of Yorkist positions along the Enfield road. The obelisk where Warwick was probably killed is just north of this. To the east of the A1000 is the hollow known as 'Dead Man's Bottom' where much of the slaughter of the Lancastrians took place. (Greater London).

The Battle of Barnet which took place on 14 April is usually dismissed as a chapter of accidents. In fact it was exactly the sort of battle that could be expected at this stage in the wars. On 13 April the vanguard of Warwick's army was already in Barnet but shortly after their arrival Edward's leading troops also reached the town. There was a brisk encounter, of which the details are unrecorded but the upshot of it was that Edward's men had the best of it and the Lancastrians retired.

At that point Edward could have occupied Barnet. However, memories of St Albans and the hazards of fighting in narrow streets seem to have deterred him and so he sent his vanguard right through the town to establish contact with Warwick's forward position with the rest of his army close behind. Warwick was disconcerted at this probing move and ordered his artillery to fire into Edward's lines all night but his enemy was much nearer than he realized and most of the shot passed harmlessly over their heads. Unlike many armies, earlier and later, Edward's army was instructed to do nothing to give away its position. Doubtless they shivered in the chill of an April night through not being allowed to light fires, and it must have been irritating to be under artillery fire and not reply, but Edward stood no nonsense; an order was an order.

The next day was Easter Sunday and Edward was up at 5a.m. It was foggy, as might have been expected in that area at that time of the year. Edward's force was inferior in numbers but was drawn up in three 'battles' with himself in the centre, Hastings on his left, and Gloucester on the right. Their position, as will be seen from the sketch map, was directly north-south m line with the Barnet- Hatfield road. The visitor will notice how marshy the ground is and how ponds produce unexpected hazards. The ground is still fairly open, although there are now a few buildings, but it is easy to visualize what the battlefield looked like, and entailed, in 1471.The opposing armies faced each other across the Enfield road, although in that light and fog they had little idea of what their opponents were doing. It is said that the armies were not quite square to each other, being aligned slightly to the right but there is no proof of this. Subsequently both wheeled to the right, but this was for a different reason. It was, of course a tendency for armies, before the days of good maps and binoculars to swing to the right, and this fact had interesting and usually predictable consequences - as we have already seen in other battles.

Both armies fought on foot, and this extended to their leaders. Nevertheless the leaders would travel on horseback to the battlefield and tether their mounts at some convenient point. This fact often led to criticism by the rank and file who suspected -often with good reason -that the horse had been well placed for the owner to make a quick getaway if the need arose. At Towton Warwick had slaughtered his horse in view of his army in order to dispel that impression; at Barnet he did not repeat the gesture, and few would have seen if he had, but he left it well to the rear; in the event his action proved fatal for he was killed trying to reach it.

There were of course other reasons for not leaving a battlefield prematurely. The principal one was the ring of knights behind, waiting in reserve perhaps, but always on hand to cut down a man who decided to take to his heels once the battle had been joined. It has a very steadying effect on a man's mind if he knows that he merely faces possible death if he moves forward but certain death if he drops to the rear. Medieval leaders had no compunction whatever about taking the sword to their own troops if they thought their efforts were not strenuous enough.

The battle began with a Lancastrian success on the right flank. Oxford drove forward on the right wing and scattered Hastings' troops. The latter were partly outflanked but quickly panicked and ran for it. So rapidly did they depart that Oxford's men streamed out in the pursuit- we have seen this happen in so many other battles- and were extremely difficult to rally. It is said that many of them were enjoying themselves looting in Barnet when they were summoned back to the battlefield. Only about one quarter of the original force were recoverable, but in the event it would have been better if they had not returned at all. While the Lancastrians were enjoying this initial success, the remainder were making little headway against each other. The Yorkists seem to have been content to hold their own till the fog cleared, for they had fewer men than the Lancastrians, perhaps 10,000 against 15,000. Edward was, of course, an opportunist who could sense the precise moment in a battle to attack, to swerve, or to split his force. His chance came soon enough on this occasion.

As Oxford made his way back to the Lancastrian position, with as many of his troops as he had been able to recover, he had to pass through a hedge which still exists. After he had left, his former position had been taken over by Somerset's men who did not like to leave their flank 'in the air'. When therefore Oxford's men returned, they were mistaken by Somerset's men for Yorkists. It was a natural enough mistake; no one could have expected that Oxford's men would now come straggling back, and to make matters worse the Oxford badge of a silver star was mistaken in the fog for the white rose of York, as worn by Edward's men. Not surprisingly Oxford's men were welcomed with a shower of arrows; not surprisingly either Oxford's men called out 'Treason' and retaliated. Oxford had had enough; his reward for victory was apparently treacherous ambush; he left the field. But more damage than that had been done. The word 'Treason', so deadly because so vague, spread quickly through the Lancastrian ranks. On both sides there were men who had fought against each other in earlier battles and trusted neither themselves nor the men standing next to them. On the Yorkist side Edward was keeping a very close eye on Clarence who had deserted Warwick a few days before and was clearly capable of further treachery at short notice.

The fighting that broke out between those of Oxford's men who could not disengage themselves and Somerset's, caused more than local damage. Many of Somerset's men began to fall to the rear, being afraid they were going to be cut off by a flanking attack. On the left of the Lancastrian line Exeter was gradually being pushed back by Gloucester.

Edward saw his chance. One desperate push into the centre and the whole Lancastrian force would disintegrate. He took that chance.

Warwick too realized this was the critical moment but with both wings gone and enormous pressure from the Yorkist right and centre there was nothing he could do. The ground to the left of the Lancastrian centre drops away sharply, and when his troops took the full crunch of the Yorkist charge that slope was their undoing. Significantly the area below is still known as 'Dead Man's Bottom'. Warwick too turned to flee, but he had left it too late. He would have done better to have died fighting but he attempted to escape and was caught in Wrotham Wood. While trying to force his way through a tangle of thicket he fell, was overpowered, and was killed methodically and in cold blood. His body was taken to St Paul's and displayed for three days before being buried at Bisham Abbey. It is possible that the monument at the present fork in the road at Barnet marks the spot where he died.

THE BATTLE OF TEWKESBURY
10 May 1471

On the day that Warwick was killed and the Lancastrian army was scattered at Barnet Queen Margaret landed at Weymouth. For several weeks this indomitable, though not necessarily admirable, woman had been gathering an army. She knew that she could count on plenty of support when she landed, for the Duke of Somerset had been organizing an army in Devonshire, and there were plenty of other sympathizers. She was met at Cerne, near Dorchester, and learnt of the disaster of Barnet. However, all was not lost. Somerset and Courtenay (the Earl of Devon) had now raised substantial forces in the west country, and Fauconberg had a substantial fleet which was threatening London.

As both Edward and Margaret knew, from the previous experience, all the latter needed was time. With time she could raise sufficient forces to win another victory like Wakefield or the second St Albans. What Edward therefore decided was that she must not have time. But it was not easy.

For the first two weeks after the landing neither side was in any condition to give battle. Edward's army had to have some rest and reward after the Barnet victory; much of it had been dispersed. It had to be recalled; there were casualties to be replaced, a new pattern of command to be installed, and more supplies to be found. It is rarely difficult to find recruits for a winning side but the problem of sorting out the good from the bad, the useful from the opportunists, is more difficult than if the army is having a difficult time, then at least you know that your men have their hearts in their work.

While Edward was resting and regrouping Margaret was vigorously recruiting. Support for the Lancastrians had always been good in the west country and now she planned to take a substantial army from that area, march it north, cross the Severn at Gloucester or a little further up, and link up with an army raised in central and south Wales by Jasper Tudor. From there she could combine forces with an army from Lancashire.

Edward realized only too well that if Margaret was not checked before she had finished her recruiting drive his tenure of the English throne would soon be over. At this point he displayed his greatest ability as a strategist and tactician. The first need was to stop Margaret crossing the Severn at the nearest possible point, which was Gloucester, and Edward therefore sent soldiers to Richard Beauchamp, the Governor, with an urgent message to close the gates and man the defences of the city. Beauchamp, with a small force could probably hold the city till Edward himself arrived. In any event he would delay the Lancastrians, and cut them off from valuable supporters and supplies in the town. Margaret realized at this point that she had delayed a little too long in the west country and on the second and third of May made a forced march to Gloucester. She arrived at 10 a.m. on the morning of the third but it was too late. Beauchamp had already organized the city defences, and with Edward hastening up to support him Margaret dared not delay to take the town. Had she tried but been repulsed she could have been attacked from behind by Edward's army which was now not far away, having come up close through one of his astonishing forced marches It is impossible not to feel sorry for Margaret, making her desperate last throw. Doubtless she should have risked everything at Gloucester but it must be borne in mind that her army was tired, was untried in battle, and not by any means ready to take on Edward's experienced and well-equipped force. Even so, Edward's army cannot have been feeling too fresh either and might well have been delayed long enough for Margaret to get the majority of her army across the river. Margaret, however, had decided this was no time or place to give battle. She decided their best course of action was to push on to Tewkesbury which was ten miles up the river. Although there was no bridge at Tewkesbury the river was at least fordable and a further seven-mile march would take them to Upton-on-Severn where the bridge was entirely adequate but could be destroyed after their passage. However, after the night march it took the Lancastrians another six hours to reach Tewkesbury, from which it is possible to deduce that there were many stragglers and formation had been lost. Edward's army was in considerably better shape although he had forced it along and refused it a rest in Cheltenham (described as 'a village'). His army was in battle formation with screens of mounted scouts or 'scourers'. From these he learnt that the Lancastrians had now reached Tewkesbury. He pressed on another five miles, and halted three miles from the Lancastrian position as night fell.

Margaret had not wasted her time on arrival, desperately weary though she, her commanders, and the men must have been. Many of them would have been too tired to eat what little food they managed to lay their hands on in Tewkesbury. The next day they were up before dawn, and ranged in position to meet Edward's onslaught.

The Lancastrians had chosen a good defensive position, a fact which is usually attributed more to the Duke of Somerset than to the Queen. It was one mile south of the town with the river Severn on the right, and the Avon, which joins the Severn here, running behind the Abbey. In front of the Abbey is another stream which runs into the Avon but curves around to the left of the ridge known as the Gastons. The Lancastrians therefore were on a ridge with the Severn protecting their right and the Swilgate stream offering an obstacle on their left. The Swilgate provided a death trap for many Lancastrians later when they fell back and tried to find sanctuary in the Abbey grounds. In the event they might just as well have been killed trying to cross the Swilgate as trust in Abbey sanctuary, for Edward's Yorkists paid no heed to religious restraints and were quite prepared to slaughter within the Abbey itself if needs be.

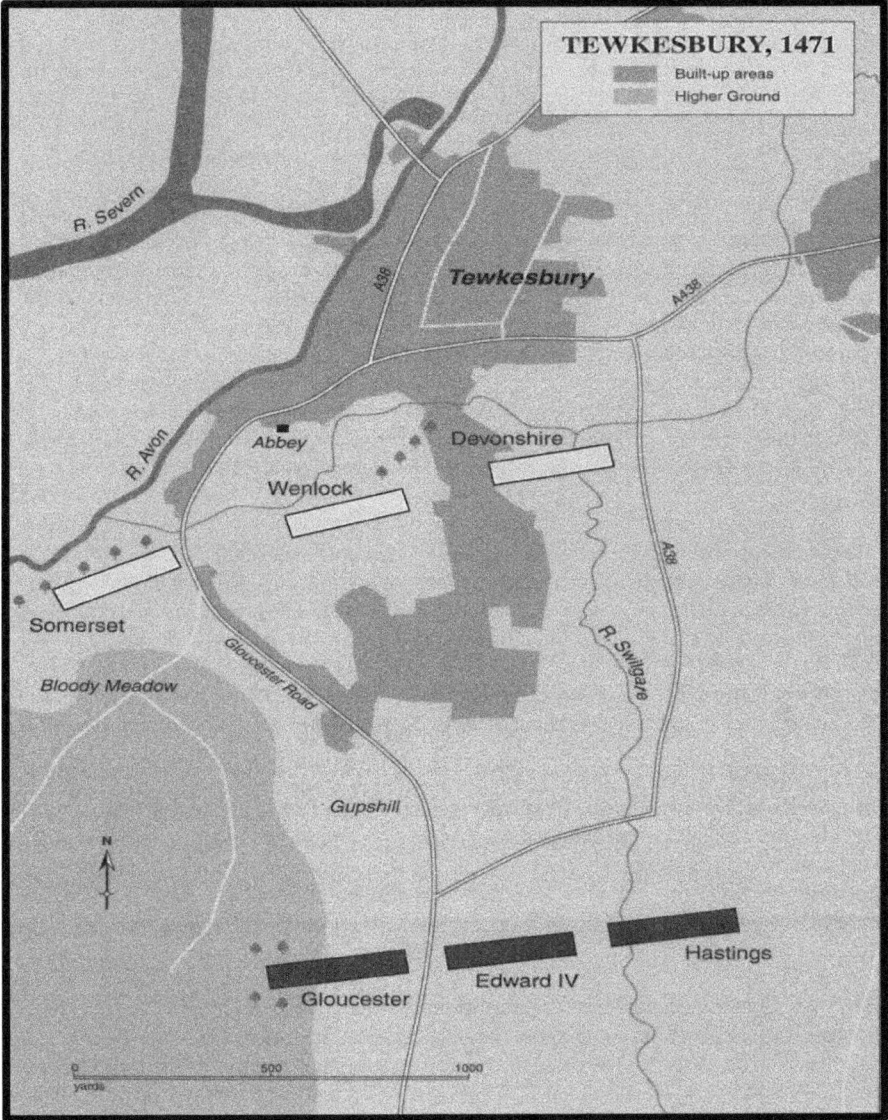

TEWKESBURY, 1471

Built-up areas
Higher Ground

The battlefield is easily found; 'Queen Margaret's Camp' is nothing to do with Henry VI's wife but is an earlier earthwork. The Gupshill Manor Inn on Gloucester Road was the centre of the start of the battle. 'Bloody Meadow' is marked, and there are various memorials in the Abbey (Gloucestershire).

In front of the Lancastrian position was very rough ground. Both armies had marched nearly sixty miles in the last three days and it was hoped that the rough ground would take its toll of Edward's men as they came in to attack, as they were bound to do.

On the right of the Lancastrian position the 'battle' was commanded by the Duke of Somerset, the centre was nominally in command of Prince Edward but in fact under Wenlock, who had been a Lancastrian first, then a Yorkist and was now a Lancastrian again. The left was commanded by the Earl of Devon. In the Yorkist army the Duke of Gloucester (later Richard m) commanded the left, which was slightly overlapped by Somerset's 'battle' opposite. On the left flank of Gloucester's position running up till it joined the Avon was a brook, now more of a ditch, which made the surrounding ground wet and marshy. The results of this will be seen later. The centre of the Yorkist position was commanded by Edward himself and the right by Hastings. Edward had, however, made an astute tactical move by detaching 200 'spearmen' - which means mounted lancers, and placing them in the wood to the left of his army's position. There they were obscured from view by a hillock. This would not seriously weaken his main front although with a probable 5,000 in his army he was outnumbered by about 1,000 Lancastrians.

The battle began with an exchange of arrows and it would have suited the Lancastrians very well for it to have continued that way. However, in a battle, as in a game, you perform as well as your opponents allow you to perform. Gloucester, wishing to get inside the artillery and the shower of arrows falling on to his position, and also perhaps with the intention of splitting off Somerset from Wenlock, pushed forward in a brisk attack. The going was slow on the very rough ground and Somerset realized that there was a good chance to outflank Gloucester's toiling battle and to come around to attack the Lancastrian rear and Edward's flank.

This, of course, was what Edward had been expecting, so when Somerset's men were stealthily moving around the hillock to the Yorkist rear they were suddenly startled and confused to find themselves charged on their right flank by the 'spearmen'. In all battles, ancient or modern, surprise has always been effective when it has been achieved. Surprise is particularly devastating when the recipient thinks he is himself giving a surprise; this accounts for the disruption of Somerset's men.

It had already become apparent to Somerset that he had his hands full with Gloucester's frontal attack, for the latter was coming over the ground faster than expected. The Lancastrian artillery, which had been dragged along from Bristol, was proving too little to check the Yorkists, who were much better served in that arm. There was apparently a plan for Wenlock to follow up the flank attack on Gloucester with a tremendous assault on Edward, or more probably, on the division between the two 'battles'. But the attack never materialised. Somerset had the mortification of seeing the main part of his 'battle' pushed back and then soon after joined by fugitives from his brilliant flank manoeuvre, which had now been cut to pieces by the 'spearmen'. To his horror and fury he saw the whole of his 'battle' disintegrate, some trying to cut right and get into the obscurity of the trees, some coming straight back through the lines and others veering back along the line of the Coin brook with the probable intention of putting first the Avon and then the Severn between them and their grim adversaries. But few, if any, succeeded. That long hollow today is still known as 'Bloody Meadow' (there is a sign at the roadside) and it needs little imagination to visualize what it must have looked like by the evening of 4 May 1471.

Somerset did not stay to witness the slaughter of his infantry. Instead he rode back to the centre where to his astonishment he found Wenlock calmly inactive. Somerset was so angry he could hardly speak but when he did find words and asked Wenlock what he thought he was doing he did not wait for a reply. Instead he raised the battle-axe that hung by his saddle and scattered Wenlock's brains with it.

Whether in fact Wenlock had decided to change sides again is a matter which has caused some speculation. His record was not one to allay Somerset's suspicions but it seems unlikely that he would have received much reward from Edward even if they had already plotted it together. The chances are that he was waiting for orders. It must be remembered that the nominal command of the 'battle' had been given to the young Prince (also called Edward) and any action likely to hazard the life of the Lancastrian heir to the throne, on whom all hope rested, would probably incur equally summary treatment from the Queen. However, right or wrong, Wenlock was dead.

What is surprising at this point is that Somerset did not take over command of this battle and drive forward. He could at this stage have sent Prince Edward to join his mother, who, by all accounts, had already left the battlefield. The Lancastrian position was bad but not irretrievable. Doubtless Edward was now pressing in the centre, and Hastings would be at grips with Devon but the Lancastrians still held the ridge - the Gastons as it is known - and the battle was by no means over. In fact the wild irrationality of Somerset's conduct at this point suggests that he had lost whatever grip he had on the day's events. He had virtually lost the battle on his own, much as the Earl of Oxford had done on the right wing at Barnet; furthermore he had strayed from a vital position. Wenlock would clearly have been at fault if he too had pushed down the slope in partial support.

However, once morale began to crumble in the Wars of the Roses, men fled while they could. These were no battlefields where the victor would behave chivalrously, where the helpless would be spared, or terms would be offered to save slaughter. The fight when it was joined went on to the bitter end. Too much hatred, too much revenge, had already gone into previous battles. The battle cry was 'kill them all'. Nobody wanted prisoners. The opportunities were there for plunder and it was easier to plunder a corpse than a living man.

The Lancastrian dead seem to have amounted to 3,000. Many were drowned trying to cross the streams and river, and once a few bodies blocked the channel the waters rose, and made room for others. There were many bones found centuries later at the corner of land where the Swilgate joined the Avon. Doubtless many of them belonged to the Lancastrian left wing who after giving a good account of themselves found the rest of the army had disappeared and they were the last to try to escape. It was no good their trying to go east, they had to find a way west across the river before the confusion of battle was over. But unfortunately for them it was sufficiently over for there to have been no chance of escape. The aftermath of the battle was as grim as might have been expected. Prince Edward, aged seventeen, who as a child of seven at St Albans had chosen the forms of death for the captured Yorkists, now met his own fate. It is said that he was killed on the field of battle but nobody really believes this story. It is more likely that he was offered sanctuary in a house, then betrayed to Yorkists who murdered him. Until recently there was an old house in Tewkesbury, with a stain on the floor said to be from royal blood. The stain might be dubious but the house and the circumstances could have been genuine enough. He was buried in the Abbey and a small stone marks the spot in the floor. His young wife, daughter of Warwick the King Maker, was pardoned. Eventually she married Richard of Gloucester who became king for two years.

Those who thought they would find sanctuary in the Abbey proved to be mistaken. It was not officially a sanctuary but even if it had been it is doubtful if that would have prevented Edward from removing his intended victims. However the Abbey had to be consecrated the following month presumably as a result of the desecration which had taken place during and after the battle.

Two days later the surviving Lancastrian leaders were taken from the Abbey and beheaded in Tewkesbury market place. Somerset was clearly the most important, but there were many others. (His brother, and the Earl of Devon, had already been killed on the field of battle.) Among those 'decapitatus' were a number of civilians whose crime was, presumably, supplying materials and munitions to the Lancastrians. Those fortunate enough to be pardoned were for the most part imprisoned and heavily fined. Queen Margaret was captured soon after the battle but pardoned and allowed to return to France. With the death of her husband in the Tower, doubtless at Edward's orders, and of her son after Tewkesbury, there was no more danger to be expected from the Lancastrians in the foreseeable future. There was - although Edward probably thought it of no account - a line of Lancastrian descent from Henry IV's brother, although one had to go back seventy years to trace it, and it was now a connection through the female line only. Nevertheless this threat had already produced Henry Tudor and Henry Tudor would in another fourteen years become Henry VII. He would also marry Edward IV's daughter and bring the Wars of the Roses finally to an acceptable close.

But all this was far removed from the blood-soaked meadows of Tewkesbury. Like Prince Edward, the most important of the Lancastrians were now buried in Tewkesbury Abbey, but there were areas where resistance would smoulder on. Jasper Tudor, Earl of Pembroke, and uncle of the future King Henry VII was still at large in Wales, there was a rising in Yorkshire and Fauconberg was threatening London. Of these the last was the most effective. Three days before Tewkesbury Fauconberg had led an army - raised in Kent- to the south of the city of London. Only unexpectedly strong resistance stopped him from entering the city and capturing Edward IV's own wife and son, as well as Henry VI who was in the Tower of London. Had he succeeded the entire situation would have been changed, Tewkesbury notwithstanding. But when he was repulsed he lost heart, and dared not wait outside the walls to be pulverized by Edward's victorious army. He returned to Sandwich, and was there allowed to surrender honourably. Five months later he attempted to escape custody and was beheaded. But by then Edward's victory was complete.

There are certain contradictions in accounts of the Battle of Tewkesbury which make an interesting study. There are also certain features of the preliminaries which have not been discussed earlier but which deserve a place in this narrative.

When Margaret landed at Weymouth (some say at Portland) Edward was taken by surprise. He had already told his victorious army it could disperse after the Battle of Barnet. He reassembled it at Windsor, but the process took a week. His great advantage was that he had good firearms, and started out well-provisioned from his base. His first need was to ascertain Margaret's intentions, and this was not easy for she sent some shadow patrols towards London to give the impression she was heading in that direction. However, Edward was not deceived for long and he set off via Abingdon to cut her off near Bristol. He reached Cirencester on 30 April, which was also the day on which Margaret reached Bath. Edward was then dangerously close, perhaps closer than Margaret realized, but she had to delay further by calling at Bristol, and collecting much needed arms and stores. Fortunately Bristol was friendly and gave her all the aid she needed. Edward heard of this move, and turned south. At this point he could have intercepted her army anywhere between Bristol and Cheltenham. However, he did not, for the following reason.

Margaret, now forty-two, was an experienced general and a woman as well. A little deception came easily to her. The only way she could keep Edward out of her path north was to give him the impression she had abandoned her original plan and was now making a dash south-east to outmarch him to London. If, in fact, she had done so she would have linked up with Fauconberg and won the war.

Instead she made a feint move to Sodbury Hill, some twelve miles north-west of Bristol. This swing to an obviously strategic point - there was a hill fort there- was picked up by Edward's scouts, and in consequence the vanguard of his army probed ahead to Sodbury. There, to their surprise they found a Lancastrian detachment and were mostly killed or taken prisoner. Those behind took back the news and Edward, deciding the Lancastrians were now about to give battle, paused and rearranged his army after the long forced march.

But Margaret had no intention of giving battle at Sodbury. With extraordinary coolness she marched her army within three miles of Edward's position and headed north for Berkeley. That night the Lancastrians slept in the shelter of Berkeley Castle and were on the road to Gloucester before dawn. By the time Edward learnt what had happened - and had doubtless finished cursing his scouts for their ineptitude- the Lancastrians were a good fifteen miles ahead. But Edward was not to be put off easily. Guessing that she was heading for Gloucester he sent messengers ahead to the governor of the city, with the results which we already know.It is said that on the last phase of the desperate march north Edward's vanguard was overlapping Margaret's rearguard. It was apparently a boiling hot day, and they had troubles enough from nature without considering the enemy. It is said however that on the last stages the Lancastrians abandoned some artillery and this fell into the hands of Yorkist reinforcements from Gloucester who were following directly behind the

Lancastrians. Sites of medieval battles are known from contemporary chronicles or grave pits; however in the absence of either it is not impossible to trace out the probably course of the action. Few grave pits have been found at Tewkesbury, and it may of course have been that many of the dead were too scattered to make it worth the trouble of burying them at central points. However, there is one theory of the battle which might be considered. It is that the Lancastrians drew up their lines much closer to the Abbey than is normally thought. This would mean the Yorkists would have to attack up the slopes from Bloody Meadow. If Somerset then charged down on them he could still have been caught in a flanking movement by spearmen. Edward might conceivably have made this move in order to cut the Lancastrians off from any possibility of reaching the ford. The reader, walking over the ground, might like to consider this theory; it does at least account for the concentrated fighting in Bloody Meadow.

THE BATTLE OF BOSWORTH FIELD
21 August 1484

When the Lancastrians were being defeated at Tewkesbury, Henry Tudor, Earl Of Richmond, the future Henry VII, was a boy of fourteen. Age alone did not bar him from high rank or efficiency in holding it. Boys were accustomed to the battlefield from an early age, and took to it like a modern child does football. Sometimes they were unlucky, as was the twelve-year-old Earl of Rutland, killed in cold blood at Wakefield, and Prince Edward at Tewkesbury, but the young Black Prince had successfully held high command in the previous century, and both Gloucester and Edward, commanding 'battles' of the Yorkist army at Tewkesbury, were only nineteen. Nevertheless, without backing, Henry Tudor was too young to be a threat. His uncle, Jasper Tudor, Earl of Pembroke very wisely took him off to Brittany to acquire years and experience in safety.

Edward's reign was not an unsatisfactory one, for most of the bigger names in the field of dissent had been beheaded, and the smaller fry had been massacred in the blood baths after Wakefield, Towton, Barnet, Tewkesbury and the like. The middle classes had tended to stay out of trouble and it is interesting to note that, whenever possible, in the Wars of the Roses, battles took place outside towns, and armies interfered as little as possible with normal commercial activity. Edward IV was therefore able to succeed to the throne of a reasonably prosperous country. His record is by no means bad although he is criticized for having had his treacherous brother George, Duke of Clarence, put to death. Clarence was said to have been drowned in a butt of malmsey in the Tower of London. Clarence was undoubtedly a nuisance; he was always involved in some intrigue or other, but his sudden and mysterious death was thought by many to be unnecessary. Some suspicion fell on Gloucester, who, it was said, had encouraged Edward to take this extreme step.

Gloucester later became Richard III and was said by many to have made preparation for that event long before. However, Gloucester, whatever his faults, and much has been made of them, was absolutely loyal to his brother Edward in his lifetime, and was a most capable soldier.

When Edward died, at the age of forty-one, in 1483, he left seven living children. The two sons were Edward, aged twelve, and Richard, aged nine. This of course meant a Regency. There were two candidates for the position, one the family of the late king's wife, the other Gloucester.

The situation was soon resolved. As the young king was coming to London for his coronation he was met by Gloucester, and taken into 'protective custody'. During the next few months a number of the young king's potential supporters were sent to the block on one pretext or another; one of them was Hastings who had commanded the Yorkist right wing when Gloucester had commanded the left at both Barnet and Tewkesbury.

Gloucester's next remarkable discovery was that Edward IV's marriage had been invalid, and had not taken place in a church at all; this meant his entire family were bastards. Confronted with this surprising discovery Gloucester saw no way out but to take the throne himself, and as London was packed with his armed retainers, nobody was prepared to suggest alternatives. Shortly afterwards the two young princes, who were now lodged in the Tower for their own safety, disappeared without trace. Nearly two hundred years later their bones were discovered under a staircase (which is still there to be seen today).

In recent years it has been suggested that Richard III's character has been made out to be far worse than it really is. This is possible but does not seem particularly likely. In his two years' reign, opposition to him mounted steadily in spite of his own skill in putting down rebellions. By 1485 most of his real or potential enemies had found their way to Henry Tudor. One who had not was Lord Stanley, who, in spite of once being arrested by Richard III, was now in a position of great power in the north-west .

By August 1485 Henry Tudor decided the time was ripe to return.

He landed at Milford Haven on 7 August. His army was small, numbering little over 2,000, but he was soon, joined by a number of useful supporters. He had a promise of support from Lord Stanley but the latter did not dare to come into the open for fear that his son, who was in Richard's hand, would be executed. Nevertheless, by the time he reached the Midlands he had about 5,000. In spite of the smallness of his numbers Henry had the heartening experience of a trickle of supporters continuing to join him .Nevertheless he appears to have been an inept commander, and a contemporary account states that at one point he lost contact with his army and spent a night away from them; they were greatly relieved to see him again in the morning.

Richard had an army at least twice the size of Henry's; it may perhaps have numbered as many as 15,000. Unfortunately for him, his commanders' hearts were not in their work, as we shall see. Initially he had positioned himself at Nottingham, ready to move in whatever direction was necessary to confront Henry. As soon as he learnt that Henry was moving across the Midlands he marched his army to Bosworth, and set out his troops in an excellent battle position on a long ridge running between Sutton Cheney and Shenton. Each army contained about one-third bowmen. By this time artillery (of which Henry had very little) was just becoming effective but the main brunt of the attack fell on the archers. Armour was by now highly complex; knights had well-made plate armour with elaborate jointing: men-at-arms had good plate armour, but the jointing was less efficient and the gaps were filled with chain mail or boiled leather. Henry had 2,000 French mercenaries in his army and these would doubtless have had the latest form of handgun.

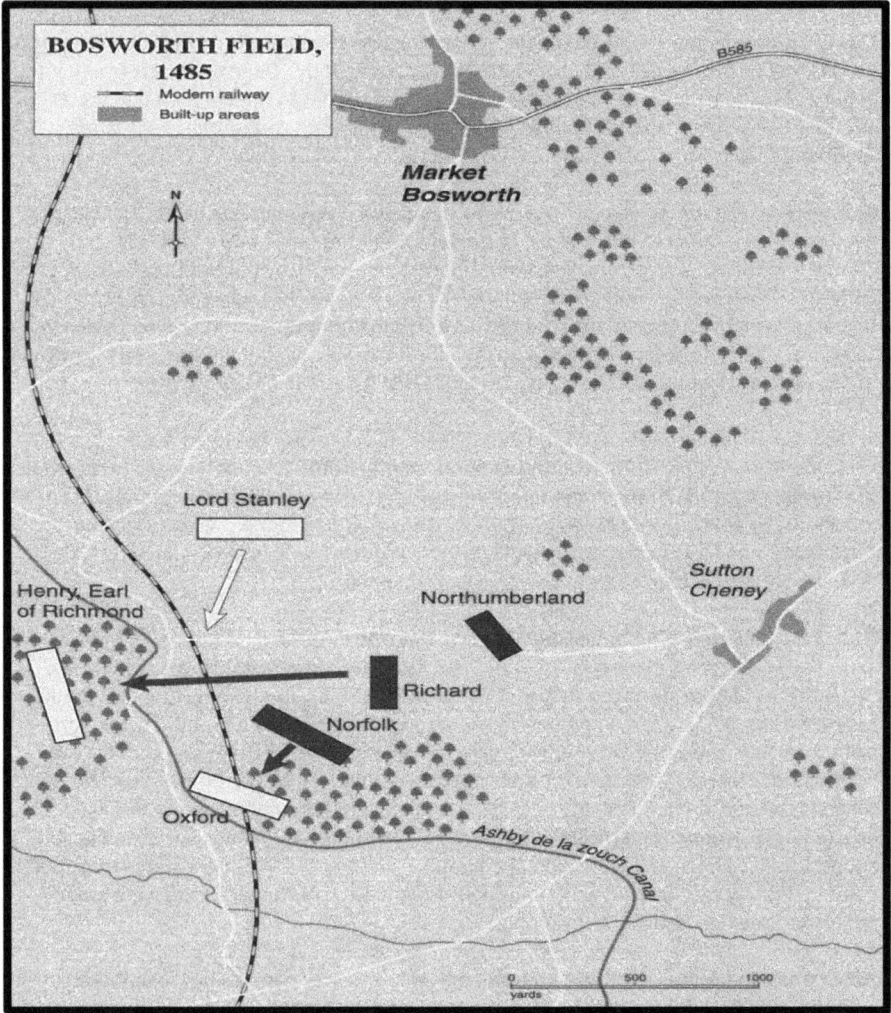

BOSWORTH FIELD, 1485

Modern railway
Built-up areas

Market Bosworth

Lord Stanley

Henry, Earl of Richmond

Northumberland

Sutton Cheney

Richard

Norfolk

Oxford

Ashby de la zouch Canal

B585

The battlefield is two miles south of Market Bosworth near the village of Sutton Cheney (Leicestershire).

So efficient had armour now become that it was the custom for almost everyone to carry a hammer. The flat side of this would be used to crack arms, whereupon it would be turned round and the point used to finish off the now vulnerable adversary.

At the Sutton Cheney end the ridge is about 400 feet high; at the other tip it is 390 and is known as Ambien Hill. The slope and surrounding grounds are wet; it was therefore a good position on which to await the enemy's attack. The crest was clear of trees, vegetation or hedges but there must have been tangled undergrowth in the marsh. Ambien Hill was clearly the key point at this stage and Richard got there first although he was not a little nettled to find that Stanley did not join him. Stanley's excuse was that he had been delayed by 'sweating sickness' a mysterious epidemic which affected England that summer.

Henry, being less experienced in war, was slower off the mark.

Richard watched him come into range but held his fire for a moment. Then, as if by a starting signal, both armies loosed off the opening rounds of cannon shot and a few flights of arrows.

From then on it was almost a chess game in treachery. Further along the ridge lay Northumberland's 'battle'. Northumberland was determined not to commit himself till he saw which side Stanley was going to fight on. Once he discovered that he could join in and be on the winning side. Stanley had 2,500 mounted infantry under his own command and his brother had 3,500 foot soldiers, so whichever side they fought for was likely to be the winner. The only man showing any real enthusiasm for the battle was the Duke of Norfolk who was pushing hard against Henry's centre with 3,000 men. Henry's centre was commanded by the Earl of Oxford, whom we last encountered fighting at Barnet when he allowed his battle to run away with him and largely contributed to the defeat of his own (Lancastrian) side. There was no question of that piece of history repeating itself. They were now in tight formation, held in by marshy land and pressed in front by Norfolk's men. Bit by bit they were forced back, mainly by sheer numbers. Henry himself had placed his command post well to the rear, and had taken no part in the fighting so far. Rather ill-advisedly he had remained static and the rest of his army had pulled away from him. Richard, watching the battle from the hill, heard this tempting news. It is said that it was too much for him to resist and that he plunged through the battle to find his Lancastrian challenger and kill him. This may be true. It may also be true that he saw the Stanleys come into the fight on the other side and decided to die in battle rather than be captured. Certainly it was at that moment that the Stanleys showed their hand. Apparently Richard hurled himself right into the middle of the Lancastrian army, which closed around him as he moved forward and swung his axe like the great fighter his record showed him to be. Unfortunately for him - though it made no difference to the ultimate result - his horse rode straight into the marsh and could not get out. He leapt out of the saddle and gazed wildly around. He may well have said "A horse, a horse, my kingdom for a horse!' as he is said to have done, before being cut down by a dozen Lancastrians.

Northumberland, seeing the way the battle had gone, did not need to enter the fight at all. Norfolk went on to the bitter end, and died fighting. Stanley, the architect of victory, was said to have picked up Richard's crown from beneath a thorn bush and put it on Henry's head. As subsequent history was written by people who had opposed Richard III his character was not shown in its best light. Whether he was more or less unscrupulous than other leaders of the Wars of the Roses is conjectural but no one can deny that he was one of the greatest of the soldiers There was no massacre after the battle; there was no point in it. The battle had lasted little more than an hour, and half those on the field had never been engaged at all.

The surrounding towns were not without their part in the battle. Near the battlefield was Atherstone on the Watling Street, Tamworth, where there was a sizeable castle, and Leicester, and of course, Market Bosworth. Henry is said to have camped at Atherstone on the night before the battle on the site known as Royal Meadow; he is also said to have acquired useful arms from Tamworth.

There is no difficulty in identifying the ridge and there is a notice by the roadside which refers to the probable site of the battle. Some say that the fighting took place around Ambien Hill; this view seems to be based on the position of the marsh. However, if the visitor follows the path behind the notice he will soon find ample evidence that the marsh could have extended along most of the base of the ridge; today, even with deep drainage ditches the ground can be very wet in August

In Sutton Cheney church there is a plaque to the memory of Richard III put up by the Richard III Society in the last decade.

There is some mystery attached to this extremely important battle. Perhaps it was appropriate that the vital battle of the Wars of Roses should be won by wholesale treachery. Perhaps Richard was the sort of soldier who makes a first-class second-in-command but lacked the ability to be a successful commander-in-chief It has often been stated that the armies of the Wars of the Roses were for the most part of untrained ill-armed men. This does not seem likely. The enormously rich and powerful barons had their own contingents and they could hardly fail to train and arm them adequately. Even the marching alone would have produced a degree of battle-fitness. Knights' armour in the fourteenth century was complicated, effective and expensive, but that of their men-at-arms would not have been cheap. Good examples of both, as well as weapons, including crossbows, may be seen in the Fitzwilliam Museum in Cambridge. It is sometimes said that the longbow was outmoded by the pistol because the latter could penetrate armour but the arrow could not. This view does not take into account the variety of arrow-heads available, some of which were as effective as a bullet. The reason why the longbow was prematurely discarded was that it required endless practice, and although this could be enforced by powerful barons - or in successful foreign wars, it was altogether too time-consuming in peacetime for all but a minority.

THE BATTLE OF STOKE FIELD
16 June 1487

The last battle in this series took place just south of the Trent, which many southerners will think of as part of the north, though the opinion will not be shared by northerners or midlanders. It is a much neglected battle but is of particular interest to those who have followed the battles of the Wars of the Roses, for it was the very last round of that bitter and bloody struggle.

After Bosworth Henry VII found himself in a powerful yet precarious position. His victory had been won for him by an extraordinary combination of allies, some of whom had fought for the Yorkists in the past. He was a most unlikely champion for the aggrieved and wronged but curiously enough that was what he was, and what proved to be his strength. Six months after Bosworth he married the daughter of Edward IV thus uniting the claim of Lancaster and York by marriage. Bosworth had not been followed by a massacre of the helpless- as had happened so frequently before, and although opponents who had been absent from Bosworth Field were indicted, they were not executed. Henry was a curious mixture: he was sober and restrained, intelligent and parsimonious, a little devious, but liable to act viciously and without restraint on occasion. This last may well be the behaviour of a frightened man rather than the sign of a sadist. There was, however, little attractive about Henry although there was no doubt that he was the right man in the right place, at the right time.

The early months of his reign saw little trouble, and his subjects seemed content to accept a rest from the bitterness and bloodshed of the past. But there were a few hardy spirits, and until they exterminated themselves in facing impossible odds there was bound to be conflict.

Notable among them was Lord Lovell. He had been a favourite of Richard m and was lucky not to have been executed after Bosworth. But Lovell was not a man to sit idle if there was any chance of winning or losing in desperate stakes. His first move against Henry vii was an attempt to kidnap him when the latter was visiting York. It failed, but Lovell was lucky and got away to France. There he was welcomed, sheltered, and encouraged by Margaret, Duchess of Burgundy, who was the sister of the late King Edward IV. Together they plotted a more thorough rebellion, and brought in John de la Pole, Earl of Lincoln. The latter had been declared heir to the throne by the late King Richard III but even if Richard had not died at Bosworth the chances of Lincoln ever succeeding him would have been slight, to say the least. It was decided - with good reason - to set on one side any claims Lincoln might have on the throne and instead put forward those of the son of the Earl of Clarence. Clarence, it will be remembered, had been drowned in a butt of malmsey in 1478 on the orders of Edward IV. His son was Edward, Earl of Warwick, and this young man seemed as good a figurehead to put forward as heir to the throne as the conspirators were likely to find. But Henry was too seasoned an intriguer to have this obvious incentive wandering around at large and had prudently put him under guard in the Tower of London. This was a problem for Lovell and his friends, but not an insuperable one. They resolved to find a suitable impersonator, parade him as the real Warwick, win battles in his name, and - when the time came - discard him and install the real Warwick, whom they would then release from the Tower. The anarchy which the success of this scheme would let loose, would of course make the recent wars look like a childish game, but this was of no consequence to the conspirators.

The plot was organized with a skill that made it almost admirable, if not commendable. Ireland had always been a Yorkist stronghold- and had served as a refuge at difficult moments such as the time after the rout of Ludford. The chosen pretender, Lambert Simnel, the son of an organ-maker in Oxford, was therefore sent to Ireland to arouse sympathy and support. It was said that he had just escaped from the Tower, and the deception worked like a charm. The Irish welcomed him as the true heir to the English throne and rallied in support. Lord Thomas Fitzgerald raised 4,000 men to support the impostor's claim, and these were joined by 2,000 German mercenaries. As Henry had secured his throne with the help of 2,000 French mercenaries it seemed propitious that 2,000 Germans were now going to be used by the opposition. The combined force landed in Lancashire on 4 June 1487 and were joined by a number of disaffected Englishmen; the final strength of the rebel force was little short of 10,000. Their first move was to get to York but after crossing the Pennines through the Aire Gap they changed course and began to move south. In the event they would probably have been wiser to have pressed on and captured York, which should not have been difficult with their numbers. Instead, they came south, possibly with the intention of capturing Nottingham. Their route is almost an exercise in strategic geography. Having crossed the main east-west obstacle of the Pennines at the best available point, they now had to cross the second great obstacle between them and London, the river Trent.

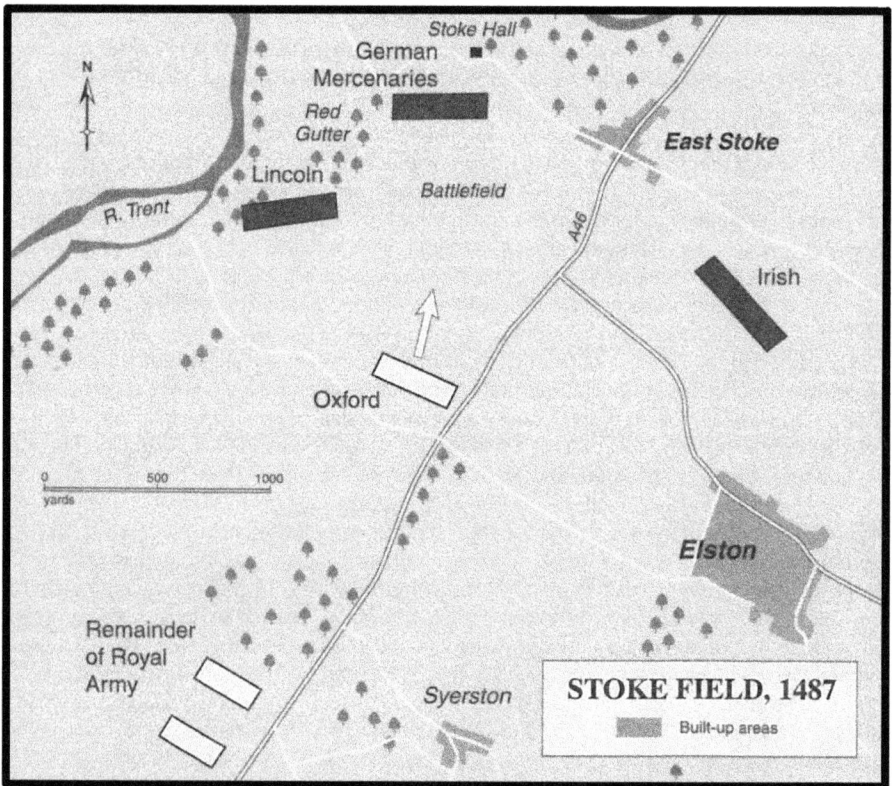

STOKE FIELD, 1487

East Stoke is three miles from Newark on the A46. There is a road which leads past Stoke Hill to the battle site. (Northamptonshire).

The best crossing places were at Nottingham and Newark but both were strongly garrisoned by loyal troops. Clearly, with an army such as Lovell had assembled a commander had to act or lose troops by desertion. Accordingly Lovell decided to cross the Trent at Fiskerton, four miles south of Nottingham. It was not a good or an easy ford, but it sufficed.

Meanwhile Henry had not let the grass grow underneath his feet. When he heard the news of the invasion, probably on the seventh of June, he was at Kenilworth. Hastily collecting as many troops as he could muster he moved north via Coventry and Leicester. After some difficulties over map reading he arrived at Nottingham on the twelfth and was very pleased to meet a strong contingent of loyal Derbyshire troops who had been brought to Nottingham to meet him; they numbered 6,000. This reinforcement brought Henry's forces up to 12,000 but, of course, numbers are by no means everything in a battle though they are a help. Henry was an astute politician but not in the category of generals such as we have seen earlier, e.g. Warwick the King Maker, Edward I and Edward IV. But, in his favour, it must be said that he lost no time in getting his troops to the battlefield at either Bosworth or Stoke. Wisely, he allowed the Earl of Oxford to make the pace and to take up a station in front of the battle. The rebel army, although undoubtedly surprised at the speed at which the royal army had come up, had chosen a reasonable position. Lincoln had placed his battle with its right on a hillock but also had the Trent partly covering the rear; the German mercenaries held the centre, almost immediately south of Stoke Hall; and the left was made up of the Irish.

The battle was a curious one. In view of its importance, for it finally established the Tudor dynasty, it was scantily recorded, and there are contradictions in the different versions. However, it seems probable that the version given here is correct, though the reader may care to consider the account given in Polydore Vergil.

Oxford in his usual forceful manner, so clearly shown at Barnet and Bosworth, pressed forward until he was well ahead of the rest of the royal army. In consequence he took the full onslaught of Lincoln's battle and the German mercenaries unaided. It was more than his troops could sustain and a portion broke and fled after about two hours' fighting. However, this apparent victory with the opposing forces slightly out of alignment, spelt disaster for the rebels, for the Irish contingent, who had so far had to do little fighting, poured forward in the jubilation and carelessness of victory already won. Their awakening was a rude one. As they swept forward on to what they thought was the wreck of Henry's army but which was, in fact, only Oxford's badly mauled 'battle' they were hit by the second and third royalist contingents almost immediately. Luck, deception, and surprise were playing their usual part in warfare. The Irish, whose courage and dash might have won the day if they had been properly used, now found themselves hammered by well-disciplined, well-armed fresh troops. Inevitably they began to fall back but what began as an attempt to re-group soon became a wild dash to get out of harm's way. Safety lay on the other side of the Trent -

although even that would not have helped for long- but few enough of them reached it. Many were caught in what became known as 'Red Gutter', named doubtless because it became a veritable river of blood that day.

This was a far greater battle than Bosworth had been. Casualties were heavy on both sides, partly because Oxford's 'battle' had been nearly wiped out and partly because the slaughter of the vanquished was so thorough. A broad river is a fine protection against enemy attack from flank or rear but a deadly hazard when an army is making a hasty departure from the battlefield. Usually the casualties are not so evenly distributed between the opposing sides. The joint total on this occasion was said to be 7,000, approximately one third of those engaged. Many of them were the German mercenaries, who fought with a dogged persistence which impressed even those who had little wish to admire them.

Some of course escaped over the river, and found a long and difficult way home. Lovell was one, but his fate was sealed. Whether he died at Minster Lovell, which was later to be renowned for the macabre 'mistletoe bough' story of the bride who was trapped in the chest with the spring lock or whether - as seems more likely - it was at Rotherfield Greys, near Henley, we do not know. But it is said - and there is little reason to doubt it - that he was concealed in a secret underground room and that his guardian was killed or captured in a search; Lovell therefore starved to death, sitting at a table waiting for the helper who never came again.

Lambert Simnel was luckier. Henry realized that there was no point in victimizing him so he made him a cook in the royal kitchens. Apparently he enjoyed the position and thrived; he was a good cook. Lincoln, Schwarz (the leader of the German mercenaries) and Fitzgerald were all killed on the battlefield.

Subsequently a few other conspirators to the throne met their deaths, deserved or undeserved. Among them was Perkin Warbeck, a young Frenchman who pretended to be the younger son of Edward IV; Stanley, who had betrayed Richard III at Bosworth but felt disgruntled at not receiving an earldom as a reward, and had supported Perkin Warbeck in his futile rebellion; and last but quite unjustified, Edward, Earl of Warwick (son of the Duke of Clarence) who had been a prisoner in the Tower for sixteen years, which was most of his lifetime.

Thus were the last threads of the Wars of the Roses cut off and destroyed. With them went an age which would not appear again. There would be battles in plenty, and even another civil war, but nothing again in English history would match that period when all the great families in England slowly and remorselessly tore each other to pieces.

THE BATTLE OF SEDGEMOOR
6 July 1685

For the last battle in this volume we go to the West country, and two hundred years on in time. Many other battles took place in the period between Stoke Field and Sedgemoor, and as many of them were fought in the north of England they are described in the second volume of this series. Most of them occurred in the Civil War of 1641-9.

The details of the history of the period between the Wars of the Roses and Sedgemoor do not concern us here but it is useful to appreciate the main events and changes during that time. A brief summary is as follows.

Henry VII, after Stoke Field, was able to settle down to curbing the nobility and refilling the Exchequer - tasks which he managed to combine. His son Henry VIII was considerably more bellicose and fought with varying success in Britain and abroad. In his reign, however, England came as near as she has ever been since Hastings to being conquered by the French.

Henry VII's son, Edward VI, was a sickly youth but his supporters won battles for him. Mary, who followed, was less fortunate; her supporters lost battles. Elizabeth had no trouble at home which could not be dealt with by an astute counter-intelligence department, and although at times in great peril finished her reign triumphant over all her foreign enemies. With her death the Tudor line came to an end and the Stuarts of Scotland - heirs by tracing the line back to Henry VII - came to the English throne. James I was not a success, and his son Charles 1 took the country into civil war. After Charles I's execution there was an interim period of Parliamentary government which soon became a dictatorship. It will be remembered among other things for Cromwell's victories abroad, particularly in Ireland where his name is still mentioned with hatred. In 1660 the Stuarts were restored with Charles II who had had enough of being an unwelcome guest at foreign courts and did his best to keep out of trouble. Even so, his attempts to make England Roman Catholic, and to once more put the throne above Parliamentary control, took him very close to disaster. The former ambition started a movement which was to have its full effect in the succeeding reign and cause the Battle of Sedgemoor. It was well-known that when Charles n died he would be succeeded by his brother who was an even more ardent Roman Catholic than Charles was, but considerably less flexible about achieving his ambitions. With this in view, the Protestant opposition to Charles II became sufficiently alarmed to back a rival candidate for the throne. This was the eldest of Charles II's illegitimate sons, the Duke of Monmouth. His mother was Lucy Walters, and in order to make his candidature more credible the story was put about that she had been secretly married to Charles. Apart from being a personable young man who looked the part of a suitable heir apparent, Monmouth was also an able soldier who had performed very well in defeating some Scottish Covenanter rebels at Bothwell Brig in June 1679. The plot to make Monmouth king made little headway during Charles 11's lifetime, but when it ended more rapidly than anyone had supposed, at the age of 55, the situation became quite different . Charles, although authoritarian and Catholic at heart, had lasted for twenty-five years; his successor lasted three James II succeeded in February 1685, and in view of his professed Romanism it seemed clear to Monmouth and his allies that the new king could have little support. In the event, they turned out to be grievously mistaken. At the time Monmouth was living abroad, in Holland, but as the time seemed ripe he landed at Lyme (Regis), Dorset in June 1685. His principal supporter was the Earl of Argyle, who had landed in Scotland a month earlier.

Both men arrived with inadequate forces but retribution was swifter in overtaking Argyle. He raised the Campbells but found no one else willing to join him. His army melted away and he himself was beheaded.

Monmouth was more fortunate, or, at least, lasted longer. To his astonishment and discomfiture few people of any standing came to join him; the story that his mother had really been married to Charles II was a little too hard to swallow. From the beginning his enterprise seemed ill-starred. It should have arrived earlier when it was hoped that the government would be sending troops north to fight Argyle. Monmouth was delayed by a variety of reasons and was lucky to avoid interception at sea. Soon after his arrival one of his chief supporters, Thomas Dare, quarrelled with the most experienced soldier, Andrew Fletcher, who promptly shot Dare dead. So great was the local indignation that Fletcher had to be sent abroad at once.

On 15 June Monmouth had a local victory at Axminster and if he had followed it up could have captured Exeter, which would have given him badly needed supplies. Instead he went to Taunton, where he was persuaded to proclaim himself king, a step which he had not so far taken. When he moved on towards Bristol he had a force of about 6,000 but most of them were rustics whose total arms consisted of scythes, picks and home-made weapons. The force was notably deficient in muskets. The cavalry were mounted on cart horses. The opposition was not very formidable but had experience and discipline. It was commanded by Lord Feversham; his second- in-command was John Churchill, later Duke of Marlborough who would subsequently show himself to be one of the very greatest of British generals. In numbers it was little over half that of the rebels but it had seventeen useful guns to set against Monmouth's four.

Monmouth appears to have had very slight idea of strategy but eventually decided he must capture Bristol. He therefore set off north-east, moving through Glastonbury (where he camped), Wells, and Shepton Mallet. However, he understood that Bristol was much more strongly defended on the Somerset side than the Gloucestershire side, and decided it would be better to cross the Avon at Keynsham, prior to making an attack on the north-eastern side of the town. When he reached Pensford, about five miles from Bristol, he heard that Keynsham bridge had been broken down, and waited while it was being repaired. It seems likely that if he had pressed forward direct to Bristol he might have captured the town, as he would have found supporters as well as opposition inside the walls.

When he reached Keynsham on 26 June the bridge had been repaired, and with a little forcefulness he could have crossed it. However, he was much set back by a charge of one hundred Life Guards under Oglethorpe, which scattered some of his cavalry. Showing even more uncertainty than ever he began to fall back to Bridgwater and during this march a number of his supporters decided to slip away and return to their farms.

Various courses were still open to him but none of them looked particularly hopeful. He could march north and hope to pick up support from Wales and the north-western counties; to do so he must first avoid Bristol and flank attacks; he also needed to arrange to feed, clothe, and supply his army with footwear if his soldiers were going to stay together on the march. Bath therefore became his next objective but Bath proved no less disappointing than

Bristol, for with the knowledge that the royal army was close at hand, the city showed no wish to surrender. Monmouth retired without firing a shot. On 26 June he quartered himself at the village of Norton St Philip and was lucky to avoid being killed by an enemy snipe who shot a silver button at him while he was standing at a window.

Norton St Philip saw a lively skirmish. Realizing that Feversham might try to attack the village Monmouth placed a barricade across one of the approach roads. As the royalists approached the barricade they were caught in a brisk crossfire from Monmouth's musketeers, few in number, but effective enough. The Royalists lost about a hundred before they withdrew, and it seemed for a time that as both armies deployed there would now be a serious battle. Curiously enough the battle never took place. After a few shots Feversham withdrew the royal troops, and Monmouth made no attempt to pursue; instead he fell back to Frome.

At Frome he met two further disappointments. First he found that a small rising meant to help him had been suppressed a few days before, and all arms removed from the town; secondly he heard that the Scottish rising had failed and Argyle had been captured.

So bad was Monmouth's situation that apparently he considered fleeing overseas, and leaving his supporters to their fate. Had he done so their fate might have been better than what eventually befell them; it could hardly have been worse. However, he was persuaded by Grey, his cavalry leader, that this idea was monstrous; and in consequence he moved towards Bridgwater. Once again he passed through Wells, and on this occasion his rabble army - which included a number of Puritans - damaged some of the ornaments in the Cathedral and stripped the roof of lead to make bullets. They reached Bridgwater on 2 July.

Much had been hoped from Bridgwater; it was reported that the town was full of well-armed and eager recruits. It turned out otherwise. There were indeed supporters but they were few in numbers and their arms were primitive in the extreme. Once again the idea of a march to Cheshire was mooted but once again vacillation prevented any forthright action being taken. As the town was completely unfortified a few ditches were dug but that was all. Most serious was the fact that so many of his men had now deserted that he now only had about three thousand seven hundred men, scarcely a thousand more than the much better-armed and trained opposition.

The very desperation of his plight now goaded Monmouth into action. If he delayed longer he might even become outnumbered. On the evening of 5 July he was told that the King's army could be seen - through glasses - from the top of Bridgwater church. Monmouth himself went to look; it was true. Feversham had brought up the royal army and it was now encamped at Sedgemoor, three and a half miles away.

Sedgemoor in 1685 was a wide plain which was only partly drained; that sort of countryside is particularly treacherous after rain. The drainage - such as it was - was effected by three main dykes, the Blackmoor Dyke, the Bussex Rhine, and the Langmoor Dyke. There was a triangle of villages at points where the ground rises slightly - they were Chedzoy, Middlezoy, and Westonzoyland. 'Zoy' is derived from old English and means an island.

The main part of the Royalist army was encamped behind the Bussex Rhine (the word 'rhine' in old English signified a large open ditch). Most of the regular Foot were stationed next to Chedzoy, and the marks on the north buttress of Chedzoy church are said to have been made by them sharpening their weapons. Similar marks are however to be found on many churches up and down the country. They were made by medieval archers who were compelled by law to practice after churchgoing on Sundays, and sharpened their arrows on the stones so that they would stick in the targets. Feversham set up his headquarters at Westonzoyland, where their cavalry, the Blues and Life Guards, were stationed. Middlezoy was occupied by the Wiltshire Militia, who were apparently of uncertain quality and uncertain loyalty. In the event they were kept out of the way of the battle.

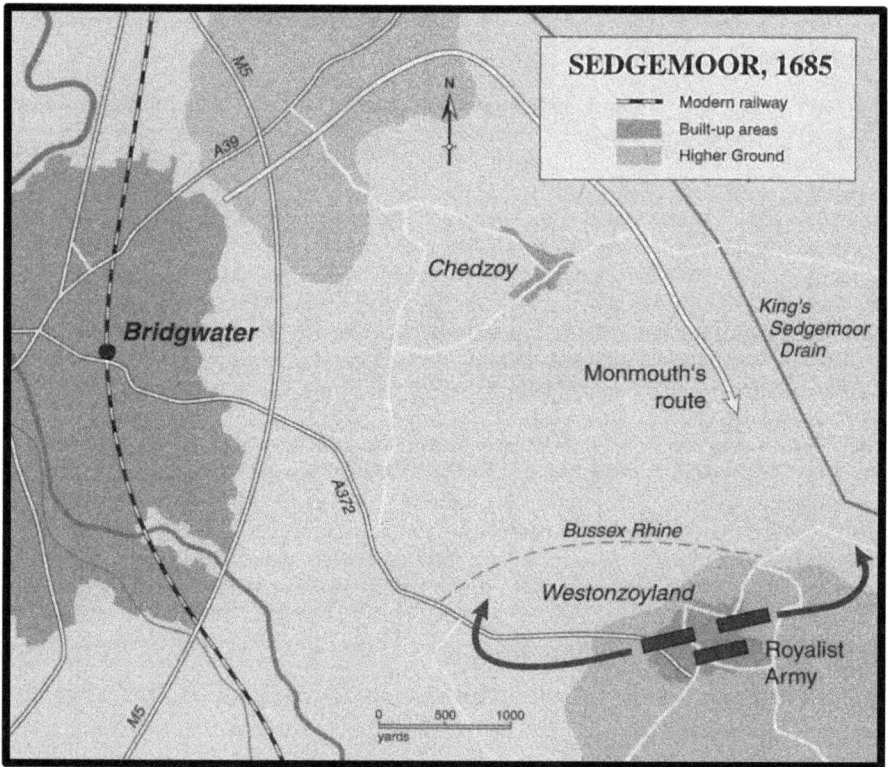

Take the A372 from Bridgwater and the battlefield is reached after three miles. The ditches are now different but the course of the Bussex Rhine, now filled in, can be traced. (Somerset)

Monmouth, now, at long last decided on action. He would attack at night and by force and surprise, scatter the royal army. It showed immediate spirit; unfortunately for him he made one appalling error. Night attacks are, of course, always a hazard. You may lose your way, you may attack your own men; it is almost impossible to know whether you are winning or losing until the issue is decided and it is too late to change your tactics. However, in Monmouth's desperate situation it was not a bad plan to adopt. And if he won there was nothing to stop him marching on London and being crowned.

Silence was vital, and in order to ensure it an order was issued that any man speaking or making any noise should be stabbed by his nearest neighbour. Silence was maintained, except for the whispered recognition word 'Soho' - reference to Monmouth's London residence.

The route was north-east from Bridgwater to the Black Dyke, which would then be followed (the Black Dyke is now the King's Sedgemoor Drain). Then by turning sharply south-east they would infiltrate inside the Langmoor Rhine. It was foggy, and much time was lost.

This was hardly surprising. The weather had been very rainy, many of the tracks were very muddy, and the moor itself was not so very different from the refuge area which had sheltered the local inhabitants from invaders in the past on account of its tangled impenetrability. It was a major achievement for the rebel army to have travelled so far and so fast in the dark. But when they came to the Langmoor Rhine some confusion developed. As the vanguard was trying to find the appropriate crossing point (a causeway of stepping stones) the centre and rear moved up closely. It was impossible - with the order for silence - to prevent it. Some confusion developed as men stumbled into each other in the dark. It is more than likely they made a noise. It is said that a treacherous officer then gave the alarm by firing a pistol; he was certainly accused of it afterwards. A more probable story is that a trooper in the Blues heard the noise, suspected a surprise attack was afoot, and loosed off his pistol to give the alarm. He then rode back to the Bussex Rhine and yelled the alarm some twenty times before notice was taken of him. But at last it was and the royal troops stood to, lit their matches, and provided Monmouth's men with a superb target.

There are conflicting versions of what happened next. Some accounts say that the rebel army pressed forward during the delay in the royalists' acting on the alarm and were making good headway when they were staggered to find an unsuspected stretch of water ahead of them - the Bussex Rhine. Other versions say that the Bussex Rhine was no surprise and in any case was nearly dry at the time but the forthright attacks of the royalist cavalry cut the rebels to pieces before the foot soldiers got to grips at all. Whatever the details the main effects were clear enough. Once vital surprise had been lost rebel morale fell. On the other side the cavalry reaction was much better and more vigorous than might have been expected. The Royalist artillery also began to play its part. The rebel 'cavalry', surprised and disappointed at the failure of their manoeuvre, refused to advance, and no amount of cajoling and cursing would make them move. It would have been better for them if they had, for at the first volley from the royalist foot the cart horses took fright and became uncontrollable. Their panic spread to other parts of the rebel army but not all. Monmouth, once the battle was joined, made heroic efforts, but to no avail. Nevertheless many of the rebels were now fighting with the desperation of men for whom all is lost, and life can mean little. Their greatest handicap was shortage of ammunition but when that ran out they gave the royal troops a hard time with their scythes and home-make pikes. The miners from the

Mendips would neither surrender nor run away, and died to the last man. The battle lasted three hours.

The concentration of the fighting in the final stages was shown by the placing of the grave pits, the main ones being near Westonzoyland and Chedzoy.

When, soon after dawn, Monmouth saw that the battle and his cause was lost, he abandoned his efforts to drive his men forward, and himself took to flight. He was captured half-starving three days later, and six days after that was executed on Tower Hill. It is said that he pleaded for his life but when he realised it made no difference what he said or promised, pulled himself together and behaved with impressive courage and dignity. His execution was bungled and the executioner took at least five strokes to chop off his head. Monmouth's venture, which, as we have seen, was an extraordinary mixture of half-heartedness and briskness, cost the lives of 1,000 of his followers killed at Sedgemoor. The Royalist losses were 300.

The horrors of this particular battle were not restricted to the battlefield for it was followed by Judge Jeffreys and the Bloody Assize. Jeffreys held a mockery of a trial at Taunton as a result of which 230 suspected sympathizers were hanged and 800 deported. Neither women nor boys were spared, and the number of those killed 'resisting arrest' by 'Kirke's lambs', the troops of Colonel Percy Kirke, went unrecorded. 'Kirke's lambs' had recently been in Tangier, where they had acquired some unpleasant methods.

Unfortunately the details of Sedgemoor are not easy to trace today, although enough remains to make it well worth a visit. The churches still stand but the Black Dyke is now part of a wider drainage complex. The Bussex Rhine and the Langmoor Rhine were filled in long ago.

The battlefield is signposted, and there is a monument, but it is not easy to trace out. There is a map in Chedzoy church.

The 'last battle on English soil' is often dismissed as being the rout of some half-armed yokels by a small efficient band of regular troops. It is more than that. It is a tribute to the courage and stubbornness of the west countrymen who, in spite of vacillating leadership, could manage a perfectly disciplined night march and then fight a far better equipped force. It is also a tribute to the efficiency of a small regular army which, though surprised and outnumbered, recovered and won a victory in the confused conditions of fog and dark. It is also a tribute to the generals, Feversham and Churchill, who handled their troops with skill and resource. Lastly, although this may seem strange, it is a tribute to Monmouth's tactical ability for he nearly won by a desperate and difficult manoeuvre when all was seemingly lost.

Philip Warner – a short biography

Historians are like deaf people who go on answering questions that no one has asked them.

Leo Tolstoy

The true worth of an individual is valued in many ways but for an historian how can we know their worth? I think many would agree that it is an ability to ask and answer questions that many would shy away from. Tolstoy would certainly agree with that and one of the finest military historians England has produced in the 20th Century Philip Warner ably matches this description.

His style is engaging but absolutely honest. He will not sugar coat when the bitter facts need to be faced. He will make an allowance for the stresses and needs of war but he will explain them for what they are not for what the victor would rather they be.

Below is not a formal biography but a personal tribute given by his son, Richard Warner, at his funeral. It's a marvellous piece of explanation and devotion that illuminates the man and his work:

I rang the Book Review Editor of *The Spectator* last week to tell him that Philip had died and therefore please not to send more books to review. I introduced myself as 'Richard Warner, Philip Warner's son'. He replied 'that is a very nice thing to be able to say'.

He was absolutely right and it does feel very nice, doesn't it, to be a child of Philip's, or a member of Philip's family, or one of Philip's much cherished friends and work colleagues, and indeed nice to have enjoyed Philip's stimulating company.

He prized above all the loyalty of family and those firm friends who he included inside that inner circle. Once you had won his trust and respect, then you were on his side and he would do anything for you. 'Families stick together through thick and thin'. You didn't let the side down. If one did, he would be slow to forgive and never to forget.

So, as his family and friends, I welcome you all here today to the Royal Memorial Chapel, to join in this Service of Thanksgiving for Philip.

Philip did not 'meekly hand in his dinner pail', as P. G. Wodehouse put it - he remained an active, alert, interested and interesting man right to the end.

He died just under a fortnight ago, aged 86, on September 23rd, peacefully in his sleep, beside his great love and companion for the last 30 years, Freda. He had gone to bed with a copy of the Spectator, in which he had written a review of a biography of a hero of his – Jock Lewes, co-founder of the Special Air Service. He had finished his day as he always did, reading a chapter from Wodehouse. He just did not wake up to make the early morning tea.

He was – in his words – 'going like a train' (an expression he had learned before the era of Connex South Central), enjoying a very busy life in his fourteenth year as the army obituarist on The Daily Telegraph (he had filed his last obit on the day before), a regular book reviewer for the Spectator, the Field, and many other papers and periodicals.

It is perhaps only in the last fortnight that the Warner family has come to realise what a special man our father was, and just how many facets there were to his life. Each of us has found out more about this reserved, steadfast, lively-minded and inspiring man from letters or telephone calls since his death.

He had special, private, individual friendships with a large number of you - but since he did not talk about himself, the facts of his life are not well known. When teaching us to box, he encouraged to 'present a moving target' - and he took this advice better than anyone. When his close friends and next door neighbours of some forty years found out only from his obituary in the Telegraph that he had been a Prisoner of War, let alone a guest of the Japanese, I realised we need to – in his words 'establish some facts'.

Philip was born the youngest child of three and the only boy into a farming family in Warwickshire, deep in the countryside, on May 19th 1914, four just months before the First World War.
Philip proudly traced his ancestry back some 500 years in the same county, loving this continuity with the past that he picked out in his first book, published in 1968, Sieges of The Middle Ages:

Standing on the battlements of a castle the humblest person feels a sense of power and grandeur. He is back in the past and feels a kinship with the original owners. In all probability this kinship is genuine, though remote. Every family that was in England in 1087 is now related thirteen times over to every other family in the country at that time; he is thus related both to the mighty baron and the most downtrodden villein.

The Warner family sold their farm in 1924, which meant that Philip had to put up with poor local schooling, making him determined that his children would have the opportunity of public school education that he had missed - never mind whether he could afford it or not.

He strongly believed that 'nothing is impossible, you can do anything, if you put your mind to it - and persevere at it'. His achievement in winning a County Major Scholarship from Nuneaton Grammar School, against all expectations, to Christ Church, Oxford, was a prime example.

Another example lay in his sporting achievement: undaunted by his isolated upbringing on a remote farm, and realising that his elder sisters were not interested in Rugby Football, he acquired a Rugby ball and a coaching book from the library: by practising assiduously in fields, he made himself into an excellent place kicker. Likewise he developed into a ferocious tackler, with a tackle bag made from old sacks and hung from a tree. This tackle bag did double duty as a punch bag, while he taught himself to box.

By the age of eighteen, he had played as a Wing Forward for the Leicester first team. He then went on to play for a great range of teams -Blackheath Moseley, Saracens, Windsor and principally for the Harlequins, in addition to two-timing two County sides, Sussex and Berkshire 'it seemed much easier to play for them both than to explain the mix-up' he unconvincingly claimed with that mischievous twinkle in his eye.

Despite irrefutable evidence to the contrary, Philip did not think of himself as an excellent Rugger player, or boxer (he boxed for the Army) or athlete (he represented his County and the Milocarians), or squash player (for the Jesters' Club). He never mentioned his own contributions - he thought only of the team's achievements and the spirit in which the game was played.

After spending an idyllic year of University sporting and social life as an undergraduate of Christ Church in 1933, he received a nasty jolt, when the authorities sent him down for omitting to pass his exams. 'Always learn from experience' he said, and did, taking care never to make the same mistake again. Rapidly finding himself a job as a prep school master, he won a scholarship to Cambridge in 1936 and graduated from St Catharine's College in 1939.

The impending war soon broke and Philip enlisted in the Royal Corps of Signals. [It gave him great pride forty years later to write the regimental history *The Vital Link,* at the request of General David Horsfield and with his collaborator Colonel Robin Painter.]

He saw action in the Far East, defending Malaya and Singapore island, where he and 60,000 other Allied troops were compelled to surrender to the Japanese and became a Prisoner of War for three and a half years.

That he felt betrayed and frustrated by the Allied command and the treachery and complicity of the politicians can be seen in his 1988 book, *World War II: The Untold Story:* 'for the British Government, and for Churchill in particular, it was an incredible disaster; to those who had been trying to make a fight of it the whole campaign had been a major exercise in frustration. The final insult was that the world blithely accepted the Japanese figures for the numbers who had surrendered and the absurdly inflated figure of 130,000 passed into history — in fact the true figure was 60,000'.

You would not find Philip making this statement anywhere else, as he would not talk about the past. He did however write about it revealingly - as in *The Fields of War* (1977) — 'When fighting soldiers eventually read or hear what was supposed to have taken place on campaigns in which they were engaged they tend to smile cynically. Sometimes they consider offering a few corrections, but rarely bother; the task, they often feel, is too large, and scarcely worth the trouble.'

As a PoW, Philip drew his strength from his background and his upbringing. He kept himself as fit and healthy as he could, remained resolutely positive in outlook and inspired his comrades with his unflagging belief that they would pull through.

To raise morale he organised theatrical productions and skits. Without props, scenery, paper, with people at the end of their powers of endurance, he still managed to put on entertainments to cheer the troops, to the complete incomprehension of the Japanese guards.

In one talk, a man who had been employed as a butler in a grand household described his day, eating meals both before and after waiting on the family 'he had two breakfasts, elevenses, two luncheons, high tea twice, and of course two dinners before absentmindly munching the dog biscuits he had pocketed as he took Her Ladyship's Chihuahua out for its nightly walk'. This to a rapt audience of PoWs whose daily ration was half a cupful of rice.

At the end of the war, Philip weighed four and a half stone, but he had survived. He set about building a new life, first at The Treasury, then at the British Council in Spain.

In 1948, with a young wife Patricia, and a newly-minted daughter, Diana (my brother and I were still ideas) he became a Junior Lecturer at the newly established RMA Sandhurst. This occupation of lecturing to young and stimulating young cadets - as well as the ideas that they gave back to him - fitted his abilities perfectly. He firmly believed and communicated that 'you could learn anything, if you put your mind to it' and that 'everybody was best at something, it was just a question of finding out what it was'. His forward leaning walk and his leadership by example appealed to cadets. H e worked here for 3l years until his retirement, relishing his colleagues, the intake of cadets, the opportunities for sport and for coaching, and the grounds.

And to a man who was committed to the principle of working and playing 'full tilt', he relished the chance that the Sandhurst academic terms gave him to use 'what would otherwise have been my leisure' for his other interests.

Thirty one years amounts to more than a third of his life. During this time, he rose to be senior lecturer, teaching many intakes of cadets about politics and current affairs.

He immersed himself in the Academy's sport: he ran the Rugby XV and taught goalkicking to the then current England full back, John Willcox. He ran the athletics too, watching with **immense satisfaction when his protégé, the Ghanaian Kotei, qualified for the Olympic high jump at the Sandhurst Athletic Ground, still wearing his track suit top.**

He loved the relaxed concentration that fly fishing on the Sandhurst lake demanded. Deeming it a suitable activity for cadets, he would declare regretfully to each new intake that – as he was both the Secretary of the Fishing Club and the person responsible for deciding who passed their exams – the lists inevitably got muddled up. This rapidly boosted membership.

It would be a matter of great delight to him to know that Sandhurst has given permission for his ashes to be scattered over the pool on the Wish Stream named after him (the 'Plum' pool), where he fished only a month ago. 'How marvellous' he said then, 'to be able to still tie on a fly and to cast a good distance – and I'm 86!'

He relished teaching generations of cadets about both current affairs and how to communicate – till his time a neglected subject. He enjoyed drawing out from each individual what made him tick, habitually asking each new student to talk for a brief time in front of the class on subjects of their choosing. Cadets responded such diverse subjects as how to soft boil an egg and how to remove the top from a bottle of champagne in one blow from a sword.

Whatever the subject, the aim was to give self-confidence to these young officers. Eventually, it led to his founding a new and now thriving department of Communications. Begun as a small section within the Department of Political and Social Studies in 1973, it now has transformed into one of the three Academic Departments within Sandhurst's training.

Philip's great break came in 1967, at a time when he very much needed one: overburdened with school fees and with a very ill wife (Pat was to die in 1971), he took with both hands an introduction to a book publisher provided by his friend and Sandhurst colleague, Brigadier Peter Young. He never forgot this kindness and determined to repay Peter's faith in him. Seizing his opportunity of a contract and an advance, he saw a way to pay for his children's education and proceeded to write two books a year 'from a standing start' for the next twenty-five years.

That was a fantastic achievement — 150,000 published words, aside from the pages he crossed out or rejected, plus all the historical research — 3,000 words a week, every week for quarter of a century. 'You have to keep pushing the pen across the paper' he would say.

Every one of those words was lovingly and meticulously typed, and retyped if he wished, by Freda. It was just as well, as only Freda could read Philip's handwriting, which resembled most of the time the tracks of inebriated and exhausted sand eels, improving for a brief period every few months as he laboriously worked from a *Teach Yourself Handwriting* manual.

Many of the fifty or so books he has written have — to his great delight — come back into print in new formats as military classics. He felt that they were good books, his earnings from Public Lending Right reflecting library borrowings showed how often they were taken out, and now even publishers have seen the light. 'Never underestimate the stupidity of publishers, Dickie.'

Though each book was a massive labour — he would just say 'toil and swink', each one allowed Philip to describe events through the eyes of the soldier at the time, rather than looking 'with the benefit of hindsight'. In the *Crimean War* (1972), he says: 'Equally full of martial spirit, strategic foresight and tactical ability are critics who have never heard a shot fired in war, never endured hunger, thirst, heat or cold, and never commanded anyone, in war or peace, in their entire lives'.

This constant theme informed his biographies of unfashionable subjects, whose leadership styles he admired: for example, General Brian Horrocks 'The General who led from the front' and Field Marshal Claude Auchinleck 'The Lonely Soldier' .... lonely he may have been, but he had the vision which allowed the SAS to get started.

This empathy with his subjects and his ability to pick out the essential character of the people he wrote about led to a life and career that can be looked back on not only with great affection but an historian's eye for truth — no matter where the awkward facts might lead.

Philip Warner – a concise bibliography

Philip wrote many books across the military range. The following titles are being re-published as both print books and e-books. Please contact us with any queries:

Alamein
Auchinleck – The Lonely Soldier
Battle of France 1940
Battle of Loos
Best of British Pluck
British Battlefields – A complete Compendium
British Battlefields – Vol 1 - The South
British Battlefields – Vol 2 - The North
British Battlefields – Vol 3 - The Midlands
British Battlefields – Vol 4 - Scotland & The Border
British Battlefields – Vol 5 - Wales
Battlefields of The English Civil War
Battlefields of The Wars Of The Roses
Crimean War
Dervish: The Rise and Fall of An African Empire
Distant Battle
D Day Landings
Famous Welsh Battles
Field Marshal Earl Haig – The Enigma
Fields of War – Letters Home from The Crimea
Firepower
Growing Up in the First World War
Guide to Castles in Britain
Guide to Castles in Britain (Illustrated)
Harlequins
Horrocks – The General Who Led From the Front
Invasion Road
Kitchener – The Man Behind the Legend

Medieval Castle
Passchendaele
Phantom
Secret Forces of World War II
Sieges of the Middle Ages
The Soldier: His Life in Peace and War
Special Air Service, The SAS
Special Boat Squadron, The SBS
Stories of Famous Regiments, The
World War I: A Chronological Narrative
World War II: The Untold Story

Zeebrugge Raid

www.ingramcontent.com/pod-product-compliance
Lightning Source LLC
Chambersburg PA
CBHW052207090426
42741CB00010B/2448